Yom Kippur
Party Goods

Tales of a Soterion Jew

Yom Kippur Party Goods

Tales of a Soterion Jew

Philip Gold

BOOKS

Winchester, UK
Washington, USA

First published by O-Books, 2011
O-Books is an imprint of John Hunt Publishing Ltd., Laurel House, Station Approach,
Alresford, Hants, SO24 9JH, UK
office1@o-books.net
www.o-books.com

For distributor details and how to order please visit the 'Ordering' section on our website.

Text copyright: Philip Gold 2011

ISBN: 978 1 84694 398 0

A CIP catalogue record for this book is available from the British Library.

Design: Stuart Davies

Printed in the UK by CPI Antony Rowe
Printed in the USA by Offset Paperback Mfrs, Inc

We operate a distinctive and ethical publishing philosophy in all
areas of our business, from our global network of authors to
production and worldwide distribution.

CONTENTS

The Meaning of the Tale
1

The Tale
4

A Brief Note on Language
8

Preface
Yom Kippur 2010/5771
12

Introduction
Four Questions
19

Chapter One
Plays Well with God
30

Chapter Two
Errand into the Bewilderedness
38

Chapter Three
Yom Kippur Party Goods
47

Chapter Four
Soterion
58

Chapter Five
Inter-Testament
67

Chapter Six
While You Were Gone
78

Chapter Seven
Kashering the Wife
90

Chapter Eight
Aliyah
100

Chapter Nine
I Don't Know Where It Is; Which Bus Do I Take to Get There?
111

Chapter Ten
The Age Now upon Us
122

Chapter Eleven
An Election of Deity
132

Chapter Twelve
Tikkun Olam; Tikkun Adon Olam
141

Epilogue
It's Better There
144

Acknowledgements
152

Appendix
154

About the Author
156

For Those Who Seek
What Finds Them

And in Memory of Raful
Died 15 December 2010/8 Tevet 5771

THE MEANING OF THE TALE

America is tired of Israel. Israel is tired of Israel. America is tired of America. The world is weary of both. Judaism's in sorry shape. The planet is worn down by humanity. And God seems, as usual, either absent, unconcerned or far too viciously involved.

These conditions are not unrelated. And unless they are dealt with – admitted, understood and corrected – only disaster awaits. And perhaps one way to begin to deal with that disaster includes reconsidering the human conception of that which lies beyond us, among us and within us.

That's the meaning of the tale told in this book. One meaning, at any rate. There are others, perhaps leading to others. To get at them, it is necessary to explore one singular idea and one singular possibility. The idea is that we are living in a late antiquity of our own, much like Hellenistic-Roman late antiquity. Or, if you prefer, an inter-testamental era, something akin to the centuries between the final historical events of the Old and the canonization of the New. The possibility is that a new sense of faith and the world, a way of faith in the world that I've come to know as *Soterion*, might make a difference both practical and spiritual. Soterion is neither a new religion nor an attempt to "reform" the old ones. It is neither a political program nor a cultural manifesto. It is, indeed, neither old nor new. It is simply a way of understanding and believing and living and doing. Therefore, it is in its own way all of these, and more.

Perhaps much more. Eventually. But you can't say everything at once. And you have to start from where you are.

This is one way of looking at where we are.

Two thousand years ago, Judaism imploded. Perhaps it couldn't have been any other way. Today, Judaism exists mostly (though far from entirely) as a black hole of malign Ultra-Orthodoxy surrounded by penumbrae of superficiality, trendiness, indifference and hostility. If Judaism is to survive at all as anything worth offering the world *once again* . . . time to un-implode.

The State of Israel has always been imploded. Perhaps it couldn't have been any other way. Today, Israel faces an existential choice. It can continue on as it has become, a bizarre combination of garrison/reprisal state, American knock-off sybaritic mall culture, religious freak show, and a politics held hostage by those who believe that twenty-first century governments should base their foreign and defense policies on Bible stories and their domestic policies on two millennia of piling up the rules and regulations appropriate to a defeated, despised, oppressed, imploded and utterly unimportant people. Or Israel can un-implode, join the world fully and offer its own magnificent potential to a humanity that needs it, just as it did two thousand years ago.

The United States of America is imploding. Perhaps it couldn't have been any other way. Those whom the gods would destroy, they first endow with invincible ignorance and equally invincible self-esteem. Today, America is at the reckoning for a half-century of imperial overreach, economic insanity and cultural self-defilement, plus other failures and evasions of longer duration. Unless America begins to un-implode, it can expect only more of the same.

For myriad reasons, from political instability to ecological peril, the planet's in trouble. That means, inevitably, so is civilization. So may be the human species. It is not impossible to conceive, on toward the mid-point of the twenty-first century, a confluence of crises more severe than any of the past ten thousand years: a confluence that will force upon us the choice so clearly defined by Shakespeare: "Up together to Heaven or down together to Hell."

And perhaps the process of facing all this begins with a reconsideration of divinity, deity and matters pertaining unto. Starting with the first great monotheistic faith. But not, perhaps, ending there.

This book is about all of this. The state of Judaism. The condition of Israel. The American collapse. The future of the species. The connections between them, and how those connections might avail.

You don't have to be Jewish to understand it. Maybe it helps if you're not. All you have to be is a human being who can read a book that requires you to fill in a lot of blanks from personal experience and belief, not always easily or comfortably. This book is suggestive, not prescriptive. So prepare to be puzzled; prepare also to make some unlikely connections and put together some odd combinations. It also helps if you're someone who understands at gut level that sometimes freedom begins when you say *No!* to the people who presume to tell you what your choices are. And then you go out and find your own. Find them or create them.

And maybe, just maybe, change the choices of the future thereby.

THE TALE

Who am I to write this book?

Who do I have to be?

A harsh and snarky answer. But not, for that reason, inapt. Joseph Brodsky, a Russian dissident who later became America's poet laureate, once stood before a Soviet judge who asked him basically the same question. Who gave you permission to be a poet? Brodsky's reply, in essence: I don't need permission. Not yours and not anyone else's. I don't need your permission to think and write. I don't need your permission to exist. Perhaps unknowingly, he'd invoked Jefferson's "unalienable rights" – rights so basic to human existence that, however viciously they may be violated or ignored, they cannot be taken away.

Who am I to write this book? Who is any of us to do anything? Perhaps just people who understand at some intuitive level that "unalienable" means more than can't-be-taken-away. It also means: rights that the individual cannot surrender or deny, no matter what the temporary survival value or convenience of such abdication. Rights that our very humanity requires that we use, no matter who we are.

Still, credentials matter. Asking others to take us seriously, to devote an hour or two of their own existence to consider us, is no authorial right, unalienable or otherwise. So please permit me to introduce myself in the preferred American manner. I'll strut my résumé.

I am an American, a former Marine with a B.A. in history from Yale and a Ph.D. in history from Georgetown, where I taught for over a decade as a perpetual adjunct. I've also been a Beltway journalist, a think tank pogue (military slang for anyone who's farther from the fighting than you are), and a deplorably non-telegenic TV talking head. I once was even requested by a campaign adviser to write a memo for a presidential candidate. It had no visible impact. Neither did the candidate. This is my seventh published book, so with that plus about eight hundred articles, columns and reviews on my CV, I guess I can call myself a writer. I also blog, but who doesn't?

I am an Israeli. More on that later.

Finally, I am a Jew. A Soterion Jew. Don't punch up your Wikipedia. You won't find an entry. Who gave me permission to become a Soterion Jew? No one. No permission asked. None given. None required. All I had to do to start to become a Soterion Jew was to be a human being who'd reached certain conclusions. Among them: It's time to say *No!* to the people who presume to tell us what our choices are. Just as war is too important to be left to the generals and the defense intellectuals; just as politics is too important to be left to the politicians and pundits; and economics too important to be left to the apostles and practitioners of material rapine . . . so are faith and faith's real-world manifestations too important to be left to the bureaucrats and thugs, the slick and the slimy, the criminals and frauds and enforcers and administrators and inquisitors and politicians and profiteers of organized Godolatry.

More on Godolatry later.

Also of importance: I am a human being who believes in that old Yiddish, and also no doubt Chinese and Zulu and Inuit and most of the rest of the world's cultures, proverb: Do not come back from Hell with empty hands. The meanings here are presented and carried as a tale, a personal tale of a decades-long walkabout to Hell and back. Painful, dreary, tragic, disastrous, untidy, humiliating, stupid, etc. etc. etc. But a lot of it was also funny, and some of it was fun. As presented here, it's a highly selective tale, the minimum necessary to move the story along. As with any telling of one's life, oblivion should have its share. Some important items are consciously omitted because they are of importance only to me. One or two others must await discussion elsewhere. In any case, the particulars of the personal tale are significant here only insofar as they reflect and evoke the lived experiences of others. I may be unique, but so is everyone else. In our various uniquenesses, we find commonality, and sometimes common cause. So if my tale is resonant, great. If, on the other hand, it strikes you as repellent or bizarre, well, to borrow from a popular song of my youth, I ain't done nothin' hasn't been done before.

That's comforting. So is another realization. There is nothing in this book, no idea, no observation, that I consider original. One of the great pleasures of coming up with some genius insight is the realization that others, often millennia ago, have reached similar conclusions. You may be wandering in the wilderness, bro, but there are tracks and trails and even occasional oases. Some of those folks from the last inter-testamental period understood a great deal. I'm in their debt.

As for those contemporaries whose thoughts and words I may have borrowed without proper attribution, I offer not an apology – inadvertent plagiarism is also a form of flattery – but an explanation. I'm writing much of this as a refugee of sorts, temporarily lodged in Israel's "Gateway to the Negev," as pissy a wilderness as I've ever encountered. I've neither my personal library nor research materials with me nor access to any significant English library. I'm also well aware of the human tendency, over time, to separate what we know from the sources of our knowledge. You know, for example, that Washington, DC is the capital of the United States. Can you recall exactly when, where and from whom you acquired this little nugget? Geography, philosophy, it's all the same. We forget where we got stuff, and to the extent that it's brilliant and/or compelling, we come to believe it's our own creation. I've tried to deal with this a bit by citing a number of authors in the book's final "Acknowledgements." But if I've omitted you or wronged you egregiously, please get in touch. I may not be in the phone book, but you can always find me via Google or a phenomenon I've heard about called "social networking," which I may try myself someday. In any event, I'll be out there in cyberspace, somewhere in The Cloud.

A doubly relevant term, The Cloud. The *Epistle to the Hebrews* speaks of Christians as being surrounded by "so great a cloud of witnesses" to their struggles and their faith. For years now, I've had that kind of feeling. "Welcome to The Club," if you feel the same. Perhaps "Welcome to The Cloud" is also appropriate.

One final confession. Before I could bring myself to write about Soterion, its faith and meanings and uses, I had to learn how to live it. Awkwardly at first, then artificially, and never perfectly. But good enough, enough of the time, to save my life. Literally. More than once. The right to life may be unalienable, but living takes effort. And luck.

If, after reading this tale, you consider yourself lucky in some personal way to have found it, that's a start. Your start. And that's the one that matters.

A BRIEF NOTE ON LANGUAGE

In this book, nearly all Hebrew, Yiddish and Greek words, whether well-known in English or not, are italicized for their first use in the text. After that, plain-type. The only exceptions are names of persons and places.

For convenience, the Jewish Ultra-Orthodox will be called by the Hebrew generic, *Haredi*, aka *Haredim*. Not all Ultra-Orthodox sects and cults would accept this designation. They differ in many ways, not least of all in their relationship to the secular State of Israel. The term is inexact, but close enough for Middle Eastern work. In no way are the Haredi to be confused with the Modern Orthodox, whose currently most famous American practitioner is Senator and former vice-presidential candidate Joe Lieberman. In Israel, by and large, the Haredi study and pray and breed and keep themselves ever more separate and pure. The Biblical term is "Holier than thou," although they might characterize it as *azut dikdusha*, or "holy arrogance." They live on government allowances, private charity and their wives. They expect to rule the world when *Maschiach*, the Messiah, comes.

The Modern Orthodox work for a living.

The word "God" presents problems, at least insofar as any use of the term structures and restricts discussion to an either/or. You either believe in "God," some kind of "God," some kind of "God by whatever name you call Him," or you fall into some other artificial, often spurious and invariably derogatory category. Atheist. Agnostic. Heretic. Apostate. Pagan. New Age. Cultist. Perplexed. Traitor. Nonconformist. Eternally damned and not at all nice. Nice enough, but also eternally damned. For convenience sake, I employ the word "God" through most of the book, and also the convention of capitalizing the relevant pronouns. Then the name is largely dropped and there is a shift with vital implications. For now, suffice it to note that Jewish lore holds that God has seventy names. God now has seventy-two.

"Godolatry" is a neologism, a word crafted to describe a situation we've been living with since the last late antiquity but have yet to designate properly. As used here, Godolatry refers to a perversion of monotheism that runs, "There's only One True God and *We Got Him*." To which is often added: "Now get with our program." To which is sometimes also added: "Or else." Sometimes the "or else" is crudely physical, destructive, murderous. But it can take other forms, as in a Christian college application I once encountered that required prospective students to certify belief in "the eternal conscious torment of the unregenerate." Almost by definition, the three monotheistic religions are Godolatrous in their institutional aspects. "Almost" because within these faiths, across the centuries, there have been many who resisted and condemned the temptation. There still are, even if their resistance more often takes the form of apathy and cynicism than principled struggle. In any case, without institutional claims to exclusive possession of a single dominating and empowering truth, these faiths lose much of their power and appeal. Given the blood-soaked history of Godolatry, and the zest with which it keeps piling up the corpses, maybe that wouldn't be so bad.

Philosophers of religion have sometimes claimed that all gods are projections of the human personality, and it may be so. But if so, we must at least recognize the empirical fact that many human beings, rather than project their own personalities upon gods wholly of their own creation, have chosen to introject – take into themselves – the religious projections of other human personalities.
Jack Miles
God: A Biography

Myth: Somebody Else's Religion
Traditional

PREFACE

YOM KIPPUR 2010/5771

Once a week, Israel shuts down. Not completely, but to a degree inconceivable in any country not burdened by enforced religiosity. Every Friday afternoon, the Jewish Sabbath, *Shabbat*, descends and the country stops, as though some kind of sci-fi energy dampening field had suddenly paralyzed an entire nation. The enforced inactivity – or rest and rededication; take your choice – remains until Saturday afternoon starts to wane. The country then resumes, as though it had vanished out of time for a night and a day but no one had noticed. Some feel refreshed. Others find it claustrophobic.

Once a week, Israel also shuts up. It's as though God had commanded, "Six days shalt thou argue and *kvetch* and do all thy carping and moaning and complaining; six days shalt thou indulge all thy rudeness and revilement. Be thou for six days jerks. But on the seventh day, give it – and Me – a rest."

Were there such a commandment (By the by, there is no exact classical Hebrew word for the English "commandment." The closest literal translation is "instruction."), it would not be universally obeyed. Still, once a week, a strange and reverential silence permeates the land. Most Friday nights that difficult summer of 2010/5770-1, from my apartment windows in Be'er-Sheva, Israel's self-proclaimed "Gateway to the Negev," overlooking Vardimon Square and Ye'elim Boulevard beyond, I could hear and feel the silence. A silence unlike any I'd ever encountered before. A blend of genuine piety, grudging respect and dreary acquiescence. A silence broken in Vardimon Square only by the Sabbath drunks and the Sabbath whores, and around me by the screaming of too many children of too many families with too many children, too many of them too deeply disturbed. On occasion, there was also jet roar from a nearby air force base. Also on occasion, explosions from the direction of Gaza. And yet, it was a silence nonetheless.

Shabbat is arguably the holiest day of the faith, the only holiday mentioned by name in the Ten Instructions. Most Jews, however, consider it lesser, if only because it comes around so often. The common preference for holiest is *Yom Kippur*, the Day of Atonement. Yom Kippur concludes the early autumnal High Holy Days, also known as the Days of Awe, ten days beginning with *Rosh Ha'Shana*, the Jewish New Year. During this period, as well as the weeks leading up to it, Jews are required to assess themselves, to utter all kinds of prayers and do all kinds of introspections, to ponder their behavior and relationships, to implore for individual and communal forgiveness.

Why God should have instructed this most self-regarding, self-centered and most relentlessly verbal of peoples to think and talk about themselves even more intensely than normal, is not entirely obvious. Perhaps a more utile decree would have been:

"All the year, day in and day out, shalt thou consider thyselves; obsess and emote to thine hearts' content. But for these ten holy days, give it – and Me – a break. Think about something else."

It doesn't work that way, of course. Perhaps it should. It certainly seemed that it should, long ugly decades ago, to a tormented American child, immersed in a repellent and oppressive transplanted East European *shtetl* (ghetto) Orthodoxy. The Days of Awe were to me the Days of Awful, the High Horrible Days. They were also annual exercises in juvenile humiliation. Jewish services do not have offertories or collections. To raise money, synagogues and temples sell reserved seats for the High Holy Days. To atone properly, you need a ticket. My family, which belonged to no congregation, was too poor to afford reservations anywhere. They did not attend themselves but insisted, from age ten or so onwards, that I go alone. After a few experiences getting kicked out of somebody else's seat, I developed the fine art of wandering from *shul* (Yiddish for synagogue) to shul, arriving just as they were letting out for their Yom Kippur breaks. Afterwards I could say, honestly, that I'd been to Poale Zedeck, Sha'are Torah, Beth Shalom, one or two others, as appropriate. No questions were asked. Wandering alone around Squirrel Hill, Pittsburgh's affluent Jewish district and personal wilderness, unable either to pray or go home or anywhere else, was never pleasant. Sometimes it rained. Since Orthodoxy forbade the carrying of umbrellas or anything else on major holidays, I either huddled in the doorways of closed stores or got terminally soaked. The experience provided good training for subsequent homelessness. Not feeling your own degradation can serve as a useful survival skill. At least until it becomes a habit that you have to break through by force of will. And can't. Or choose not to.

But now the degradation is gone. So is the derision. What has replaced them is far more somber and purposeful. It is also not according to the standard Jewish script.

In Judaism, a *Ba'al-T'shuva* is someone who returns after long alienation or indifference. "Ba'al" means "master." "T'shuva" means both "repentance" and "return." The same word, or one closely related, means "answer." One who returns is more than a penitent. He or she has found the answer. That answer, presumably, is some form of tradition, most probably some form of Orthodoxy, some form of acceptance of that which is, that which has been crafted and offered to you by others.

That one can be Ba'al-T'shuva, a master of penitence, and return for entirely different reasons is not generally acknowledged.

Perhaps it should be. One of the meanings of the name "Israel" is "Struggles with God." Supposedly, the Ba'al-T'shuva ends alienation with some form of submission, total or merely initial. Struggle's over, more or less. One way or another, the match ends in a forfeit. Your forfeit.

Sometimes, however, the answers that generate return also mandate a new kind of strife. By origin, the word "orthodox" is a Christian term. It comes from the Greek and means literally, "straight-thinking." By contrast, "heresy" derives from the Greek for "choice" or "choosing." By definition, heretics are those who choose something other than orthodoxy.

Some members of the Chosen People, as the cliché has it, "choose to be Chosen." Others choose strife; Judaism has a long tradition of challenging the divine from a stance of faith. Apostates leave. Heretics sometimes choose to stay. Or to return.

Am I a heretic? Only by the definition of those who take the stance: We can't be right unless everybody else is wrong. Judaism has always been thus.

Shabbat is holy. Yom Kippur is holy. When the two coincide, they form indisputably the holiest day in Judaism. The two coincided in the year 2010/5771. The Christian 2010 AD, *Anno Domini*, in the Year of Our Lord (Or CE, of the Common Era) is marked from the birth of Jesus. The dating is now conceded to be a bit off, due amongst other things to the sloppy arithmetic of Dionysius Exiguus, the sixth-century monk who worked up the Church's liturgical calendar: the system that would free Christianity of yet another congruence with an increasingly despised Judaism. The Jewish 5771 is marked from the God of Israel's creation of the universe. Also a bit off.

Friday evening, 17 September 2010. The tenth day of *Tishrei*, first month of the Jewish lunar calendar. Nearly midnight. My radical feminist two-war veteran journalist/author horse-woman/weight lifter former Army reserve officer quasi-pagan *shikse*, i.e., deliciously Gentile, wife is asleep in our bedroom. Erin's the product of a family that renounced its Judaism when they came to America several generations ago, but couldn't erase the ancestral ties merely by trashing the documents. Six hard months have passed since we first came here from America with eighty-six dollars to our names, the wreckage of our professional lives as writers and the determination to accomplish certain things. These are getting done. Slowly, fitfully, too often sloppily, but getting done. We're still writing for the American market. But we're also looking for Israeli work and starting our own little company. The State of Israel, to whom we owe our physical survival, will find us useful soon enough. More useful than we could have been in the country that America has permitted itself to become.

Israel. Land of Opportunity. Who knew?

We're adjusting. We're learning Hebrew, even if Erin still considers it less a language than a collective psychotic delusion: a common initial response. Soon enough, we'll be productive. But not tonight. This evening I just look out the window of the flat's second bedroom, for now my study. Five or six adults are talking loudly down in the square. Two children are with them, screaming and dragging a skateboard about. They seem to be some sort of family, although why they're out so late isn't clear. The night's few drunks, perhaps courteously, stay out on the street. An occasional female scream comes from that direction, but nothing like the ordinary shriek-and-holler invitations to customers regular, occasional and potential. Then there is silence.

Blessed be He Who sendeth the drunks home early and giveth the whores the night off.

The adults in the square, after a bit more shouting at each other and into their cell phones, depart. The children follow noisily, unwillingly. Then the silence becomes total and holy.

There is wine on my desk. Good Israeli wine. Mogen David this is not. The old canard about Israeli vintners turning wine into water lost its applicability long ago. There's mediocre salami from a local Russian gastronome, too much gristle and most likely not Kosher. There's a preposterously expensive canister of jalapeño Pringles, imported from America.

Yom Kippur Party Goods.

Not much. Also not much of a party, especially since Yom Kippur requires a night and a day of fasting. But a year ago, it was the sudden, accidental, Internet-induced notion of Yom Kippur Party Goods and subsequent odd combinations that reified the process of deciding to leave an America that had neither room nor use for us and was in fact quite willing to let us die in the street. We'd been discussing *Aliyah*, emigration to Israel – the word means, literally, "Going up" – for years. Yom Kippur Party Goods gave it meaning. Destitution and homelessness gave it urgency.

So we're here. Will we ever return to America? It is to be hoped that we will. Perhaps we'll find ourselves, reasonably prosperous once again, dividing our time. The State of Israel will always have our gratitude, our love, our determination to take such responsibility for its welfare as might come our way. If it turns out that we spend the rest of our lives in this difficult, imperfect, vicious and enchanted place, we won't be unhappy. But America, that difficult, imperfect, vicious and enchanted place, still matters greatly. It could not be otherwise.

Midnight has come and gone, unnoticed. *Kol Nidre*, the evening service, ended hours ago. Kol Nidre: All Vows. The Yom Kippur liturgy proclaims that all vows taken under duress are null and void. I've taken a few of those vows under great duress, psychological and physical. I voided them out myself. That was enough.

The wine is nearly gone. The snacks – no more. There's a difference between symbolism and juvenile acting out. You're beyond all that. Some things need to be taken respectfully, even if you don't share them. But what do you share with anyone, anymore? What can you share?

Blessed are those who, refusing to accept the choices offered them or forced upon them, go out unto the wilderness to find their own. To find them or create them. And then to bring them home.

And blessed is any deity with the decency to let them do so, and the wisdom and courage to share in the finding and in the creation.

I'm an American. I'm an Israeli. I'm a Jew. A Soterion Jew. This is the tale I would like to tell you. It neither obligates nor forces you to anything. How could it? Read on if you like. Do with it as you will. And whatever choices you choose – for in the end we all must choose and refusal to choose is itself a choice . . .

Be well.

INTRODUCTION

FOUR QUESTIONS

Law without enforcement power isn't law. Law without enforcement power is opinion. But opinion may have great influence and generate prerogatives, including the right and power of the "straight-thinking" to tell you what your choices are.

Today, there is nowhere on earth where *Halakha*, Jewish law as it has evolved these past two millennia-plus, is enforced by the secular State. Not even in Israel. The Rabbinate controls marriage, divorce and questions arising from that age-old fundamental question, "Who is a Jew?" and thus eligible for Israeli citizenship. The decisions of rabbinical courts in these matters may be enforced by the State. The Rabbinate and the religious political parties also endlessly demand and often receive special dispensations and allowances, and influence governance on everything from public transit and the status of women to foreign and defense policies. Most Israelis, who consider themselves secular, dislike this arrangement. But the Ultra-Orthodox, roughly a ten-percent minority (for now; they breed with gusto and recruit with zeal) enjoy an influence utterly disproportionate to their numbers. Some of that influence derives from respect for tradition, even among the alienated and the lapsed. Much derives from Israeli coalition politics; in a multi-party parliamentary system, small factions often charge high prices for their participation in coalitions and other forms of co-operation. The religious always have. And some derives from the increasing Ultra-Orthodox penchant for violence and the desire of the government to appease them, at least until some more pressing problems are attended to and the country maybe someday gets around to writing itself a constitution

The Ultra-Orthodox are far from a homogeneous group, and as given to intramural disputation as any other set of cults and fanatics, especially regarding Israel's religious legitimacy. For present purposes, we'll refer to all Jews more extreme than the Modern Orthodox as *Haredi*, a Hebrew word sometimes roughly translated, "Those Who Tremble before God." The actual plural is *Haredim*; Haredi can be both an adjective and a noun.

So what do Those Who Tremble before God – disparaged by many secular Israelis as "The Nervous Ones" – do all day?

They pray. They study. They breed. Most avoid military service and productive work. Rabbinical students, a term that can be expanded to include nearly every draft-age male poring over the ancient texts in some hole-in-the-wall *yeshiva* (Ultra-Orthodox academy) somewhere, are draft-exempt. According to official estimates, over seventy percent of adult male Haredi are unemployed by choice. Haredi live apart in closed communities or enclaves, on government allowances, private charity and their wives. They also riot over anything that offends them, from female immodesty as they define it to autopsies (forbidden) to Jerusalem parking lots that the municipal government dares to keep open on Shabbat.

Most of all, they await the coming of *Maschiach*, the Jewish Messiah, and *Ha'Olam Ha'Ba*, The World to Come. Judaism holds no consensus on what The World to Come will be like. But the Haredi know one thing. They'll be in charge.

Some, while waiting, prefer not to wait. They speak of creating a "Torah-based" society, a Jewish theocracy. Current indications of what this society might look like include sex-segregated public buses (women to the rear), refusing to rent to Arabs and denying Jewish burial to immigrant soldiers who died in service to Israel, but whose Jewishness is deemed inadequate. In 2010, a certain Rabbi Yitzhak Shapira published a book, *The King's Torah*, suggesting that killing Gentiles, including children, who pose no danger but who might, is acceptable. And several years ago I read of one rabbi, name now mercifully forgotten, who averred that a "Jewish Taliban" might be nice.

Some of the Haredi – I've met a few – are good and decent people who have chosen this way of life because it speaks to them. Others choose it because they wish for lives wherein every detail is regulated and all vexations may be referred to others for solution. Some are trapped there and, unwilling or unable to leave, run up the psychiatric and the suicide stats. Others are tyrants-in-waiting.

It is hard to avoid the conclusion – many have reached it – that Haredi Judaism and Islamism are, in matters of outlook, style and intent, converging. Such is the nature of Godolatrous faith. It cannot be otherwise, when power beckons.

Why mention this here? Because it raises the first of four questions. And also because of a personal reaction to *Ha'Kotel*. The Wall.

The Haredi control The Wall. But they cannot control its evocation, not just of Roman oppression and catastrophe, but of the Jewish fanaticism that made the disaster possible. As Amos Oz, the great Israeli writer, put it so well in his dated but still relevant *In the Land of Israel*: "The Jewish people has a great talent for self-destruction."

And it ain't over yet.

Judaism has only one universally-acknowledged holy city, Jerusalem. Safed, Hebron, Tiberias, Vilna, Odessa, New York, Miami Beach matter less. Judaism has only one universally acknowledged holy shrine: the Western Wall, once hideously known as the Wailing Wall. The Wall was originally a retaining wall of the Second Temple's platform, and is revered absolutely. Of Judaism's six fast days, four relate to the destruction of the two Temples, the Second especially, the one destroyed by the Romans in 70 CE along with the Jewish State. Nineteen centuries later, Israel wrested the Old City of Jerusalem from Jordan, which had seized it in 1948 and barred all Jewish entry, after a horrifically bloody battle. Today, Jews come from everywhere to pray at The Wall and to leave their requests on pieces of paper wedged between the stones. There are even companies that provide the insertion service for Diaspora Jews unable to come themselves. Just fax us your requests. Properly observant and pious employees will tend to the rest. Prayers included at no extra charge. Credit cards accepted.

Jews who visit The Wall for the first time often speak later of the intensity of their experiences, their sudden closeness to the Jewish past, the Jewish people and the God of both. My first experience, in 2010, was also intense, a moment when decades of study and pondering suddenly coalesced into a single explosion of rage.

You can access The Wall in two ways. There may be more. You can come in through the Dung Gate, from a noisy commercial street crowded with tourists, cars, buses and souvenir/falafel stands. Or you can come down from an arcade of shops, religious goods stores, cafes and souvenir/falafel stands. There are the standard security check-points, plus cameras, antennae and other items mounted all around. You enter the plaza constructed after the Six Day War to "let The Wall breathe" and to accommodate the crowds that have been coming ever since. The first thing you notice: how small it all is. The Wall itself, the plaza, the entirety of it. Like all of Israel, it's always smaller than you expect.

You approach The Wall itself. There's a long partition perpendicular to it, separating men and women. If a man moves toward the women's section – a mistake I inadvertently made, walking my wife toward that side – a dozen people, mostly women, sternly and fearfully warn you away. If a woman even begins to approach the men's side, she can expect to be physically barred, perhaps removed by force, and perhaps assaulted. Women have been physically attacked there before, and also for praying "immodestly" on their own side.

"Separation is a blessing." Or so the Haredi tell us.

Obedient, I went to the men's side, my *kipa*, my skull cap, firmly on. An obese little bearded man in the standard ill-fitting black and white, black jacket and trousers, white shirt, no tie, black hat, approached me. He was carrying a *tallis* and t*ephillin*, the former a ritual prayer shawl, the latter small wooden boxes on leather straps, worn on head and arm during prayer. He gave me to understand that he wanted me to pray thus arrayed, and would lend – rent? – them to me. Instruct me also, should my knowledge of such matters prove inadequate. I shrugged him off. Another, identically attired but empty-handed, approached me and began to ask for money. I dismissed him with a conveniently American *Eyn Ivrit*, No Hebrew, and went to The Wall. I stared at the stones. I refused to touch them. I said no prayers. I had nothing to insert. I did, thought, felt nothing. Then a sudden emotion possessed me.

How dare they?

How dare they presume to control this place when it was their brand of faith, their brand of culture and of politics that caused the disaster in the first place, and may yet cause another?

How dare they?

Nineteen centuries ago, Jewish fanaticism, Jewish social stratification and economic inequality, Jewish mutual oppression, exploitation and stupidity provoked an utterly unnecessary rebellion against Rome that led to an utterly unnecessary and savage civil war and an utterly catastrophic Roman reconquest. The Talmud says that God did not permit the destruction of the Temple and the State because of impiety. He permitted it because of *sinat hinam*, usually translated "baseless or groundless hatred" between Jews. The translation is lacking. A more accurate rendering would be "pure hatred," especially the purity of hatred that the Ultra-Orthodox of all religions and ideologies so zestfully reserve for the rest of the world, and inflict upon it whenever they get the chance. To me, as perhaps to many others,

The Wall is less a memorial to faith across the millennia, less a reminder of Gentile persecution, than of deadly intramural hate. Nineteen centuries ago, the Jews of Jerusalem slaughtered each other, even with the Romans at the gates. Today, sinat hinam in its various forms, from internecine religious intolerance to Israel's stance before the world, threatens to destroy again.

There's an axiom of discourse. Who frames the debate, determines the debate. For over two millennia, the Zealots of religion and politics have framed the debate over Judaism. Even their most ardent foes, from the philosophers of the *Haskala*, the Jewish Enlightenment, to the architects of Reform Judaism and secular Zionism, have fought and argued as much against the rabbinic/Halakhic heritage as in favor of creating something new. Sadly, that "something new" has never quite come about, only a series of shaky compromises with Christian and secular culture and one great accomplishment – Israel – that must contend with this latest resurgence of political and religious fanaticism, as well as with its own dilemmas of governance and culture.

Two thousand years ago, the rabbis won. And it matters not at all whether their putative ancestors, the *Pharisees*, favored the Roman War or not. For two millennia, the rabbis have ruled, not least of all because Christian and Muslim oppression gave them the Jewish people as a captive audience. And Judaism ever since has consisted either of submitting to or rebelling against them, or ignoring them as best you can – and of being whipsawed between the *rebbes* and the *goyim*, century after dreary century.

But sometimes freedom begins when you say *No!* to the people who presume to tell you what your choices are, even if they've been at it forever. So it must be asked: What might a post-rabbinical, a post-Halakhic Judaism, a Judaism in which rabbis were pastors and advisers only, and in which Halakha held the status of tradition only entail, for the Jewish people and perhaps the world?

And thus the first question of four. If you can't (as Ike so sagely put it) face the future by marching backwards into the past, and the old sinat hinam remains as deadly as ever . . . what next for Judaism as a faith in a world for which it might once again assume some responsibility?

The question matters. Non-Haredi Judaism is a dying faith around the world, especially in America. It seems that, whenever given the choice, the vast majority of Jews want nothing to do with Orthodoxy. Meanwhile, Judeophobia is enjoying a metastasis of its own, this time as toxic anti-Israelism. So this "What Judaism Now?" question also matters intensely to the State of Israel. In the classic Zionist formulation, as expressed in Theodor Herzl's *The Jewish State*, there was no room for Zealotry:

"We shall keep our priests within the confines of their temples in the same way as we shall keep our professional army within the confines of their barracks. Army and priesthood shall receive honors high as their valuable functions deserve. But they must not interfere with the administration of the State which confers distinction upon them, or else they will conjure up difficulties within and without."

Of course, for a variety of reasons it didn't happen that way. But the principle remains apt. Today, Israel balances between a self-destructive quest for religious purity and an equally self-destructive desire to become just another deliciously decadent Mediterranean fleshpot/consumer culture So it must be asked: What might a post-rabbinical, post-Halakhic, perhaps even post-militarized Israel look like – a country that offers its people more choices than the *mikva* (a ritual bath) or the mall? Could it survive and take its rightful place in the world, recovering Herzl's hope that "whatever we attempt to accomplish there will react powerfully and beneficially for the good of humanity"?

Only Israel can answer that question. But to a great extent, the answer depends on America. Not on America as rich and indulgent Uncle Sammy. Nor on America as the honest broker who ends the bloodshed. For America is no longer the first and cannot be the second. America's imploding and the implosion will continue until either catastrophic collapse or fundamental change. Which gives rise to the third question: Can Israel and the United States, two countries that have lost their way, help each other to find it again? Today, the country that Israel has become can no longer speak to the country that America is becoming. But what of the country that Israel could become and the country that America must become?

Which leads to the final question. If it is true that a confluence of crises and disasters is now coming upon the planet, and if it is conceivable that toward the midpoint of this century, maybe sooner, they will converge into a fundamental threat to human civilization and perhaps humanity itself . . . what role might a redeemed Israel and a reformed America play *together* in such a situation? Or would it be more appropriate to speak of a reformed Israel and a redeemed America?

And thus, four questions:

What might a post-Halakhic/post-rabbinical Judaism offer the world?

What might a brilliantly post-Zionist/post Haredi Israel offer the world?

What might such a Judaism and such an Israel offer an America descending into its Time of Troubles, and what might it receive in return?

And what might they – we – do together to prevail against the age now upon us?

A possible clue lies in the way of faith and living that I've come to think of as Soterion. As already noted, you don't have to be Jewish to understand it. Maybe it helps if you're not. But you do have to be willing to give me an hour or so of your time to tell you a tale. Don't worry if the tale seems a bit non-linear, perhaps disjointed, riddled with lacunae, incomplete. Many years ago, whilst teaching at Georgetown University, a student came up to me after a lecture.

"You say something," she said, "and it raises a question. Then you say something else and it raises another question. After a while, all I've got are questions."

"Good. That means I'm doing my job."

The young woman smiled. "You know, I just can't hate you the way I should."

And you don't have to be Jewish to understand that.

Consider the work of God;
who can make straight what He has made crooked?
Ecclesiastes 7:13

So often times it happens
That we live our lives in chains
And we never even know
We have the key.

The Eagles
"Already Gone"

CHAPTER ONE

PLAYS WELL WITH GOD

"*Oy*, Fannie, he prays with a Jewish heart."

Or so my mother told me that Menachem Ruttenberg had said.

Menachem Ruttenberg, back in the early 1960s, was, if memory serves, the principal of the Yeshiva Achei Timimim in Pittsburgh. My mother worked there as a book-keeper and had arranged for me to spend several summers getting simultaneously under-day-camped, over-indoctrinated and perpetually mocked by the year-round yeshiva *bokherim* (students) as a *shagutz*, a non-Jewish boy, due to my lack of *payos*, long side-locks, and *tzitzes*, the fringed undershirt usually worn with fringes showing. Mr. Ruttenberg also taught at the Hebrew Institute of Pittsburgh, which my mother had arranged for me to attend on scholarship four afternoons a week after school, for at least as long as I'd been alive. At the time of Mr. Ruttenberg's approbationary comment I was twelve, condemned also to waste four hours every Sunday morning at "Breakfast *Minyan*," an educational prayer service for boys to be *Bar Mitzvah* that year. A minyan is at least ten adult Jewish males together at prayer; a bar mitzvah is the ritual entry into adulthood at age thirteen. "Bar" means "son." "Mitzvah" translates as "commandment" but also may mean "good deed." The purpose of Breakfast Minyan was to prepare little Yidls for their upcoming transformation into big Yidls by staging a full synagogue service for them alone. We learned how to don our tallis, strap on our tephillin, stand up sit down stand up sit down stand up sit down, sway back and forth and pray pray pray. The more astute among us had already mastered the fine art of mumbling in what sounded like Hebrew.

Others no longer even bothered to turn the pages of their prayer books. We were not, as a rule, enthused.

That morning, I was more than usually unpleasant. I was irritated and bored. The leather straps were cutting into my arm when they weren't falling down and my little knitted kipa, my "itsy bitsy teeny weeny blue and white embroidered beanie" (adapted from a then-popular song about an itsy bitsy teeny weeny yellow polka dot bikini) wouldn't stay on for lack of the requisite fasteners, women's bobby pins. I was also hungry. As Fuzzy, aka Old Man Abrams, the geriatric *schlumpf* who ran the place with his son, Dr. Abrams, aka Fuzzy, Jr., had ordained it, Minyan was followed by Breakfast. This consisted of whatever was left over from the *Kiddush* the day before, the Shabbat post-morning service brunch provided by the parents of that week's Bar Mitzvah boy. The Hebrew Institute had no synagogue of its own. But it rented space to the Young People's Congregation, a collection of Modern Orthodox business and professional types, some of them very impressive, who didn't want the burden of their own building, i.e., their own mortgage, upkeep expenses and the intramural squabbles such expenses always generated. As part of the deal, any Hebrew Institute boy whose family didn't belong to a synagogue, usually because of poverty, could be Bar Mitzvah there.

I would be – an embarrassment I wasn't looking forward to. But this morning my mind was on food. Some Sundays you made out. Real lox, still-fresh bagels, herrings and fishes and cheeses and meats. Meat and dairy were, of course, served on separate tables and woe betide the lad whom the ardently-*fressing* Sunday school faculty apprehended in the act of mixing the two. Other Sundays you were lucky to come away with a little carton of chocolate milk. Either way, it was a Breakfast Minyan ritual to get from Minyan to Breakfast with as little time as possible elapsed between the two. Naturally, the boys who were most adept at velvet-bagging their tephillin, kissing their tallis good-bye and running through human and vehicular traffic from the old building to the new one across the street, got there first. Indeed, getting out of the gear had become something of a preliminary contest, with the singing of *Eyn Kelohanu* ("There is None Like unto Our God"), one of the final prayers, the signal to begin. Fortunately, it was a zippy number and you could spin off your straps to the rhythm.

In sum, Breakfast Minyan was three hours of excruciating boredom, followed by a pack feeding frenzy. This Sunday, however, would be different. Two hours on, Mr. Ruttenberg entered to inspect. In truth, he was a pretty good guy. Unlike the rest of the yeshiva hierarchy, he was clean-shaven and well-dressed. There were stories about his *Haganah* (pre-1948 Jewish semi-underground defense force) exploits before he came to America from what was then Palestine. One tale held that he barely escaped. The British had a leftover death sentence on him from his wartime days with the Palestine Brigade, when he'd struck an officer who tried the standard insult on the wrong Yid. The sentence had never been carried out (obviously) but may have been still, to coin a phrase, hanging over him, should his Zionist activities result in arrest. Knowing Mr. Ruttenberg, such tales were plausible. Better documented was his unavailing opposition to firing the yeshiva's school bus driver, a young black man who'd recently been charged with statutory rape. "But the girl was willing . . ." he'd kept repeating, even after the fellow was gone.

Deep down, I suspect, Menachem Ruttenberg enjoyed chain-jerking the yeshiva and Hebrew Institute power structures. But only to a point. With four young children, he needed both jobs. And he had no nastiness within him. He was a man very much at peace with himself, his people and their faith. He played well with Jews and with God.

I liked Menachem Ruttenberg, but had been disappointing him of late. At my mother's request, he'd been having me over to his house for Saturday lunch, followed by study sessions, lest I experience a day without *Yiddishkeit* (the fine art of Jewishness). Study ended when he retired to the bedroom with his lively wife and I amused the kids for an hour or so. In retrospect, I realize that I was providing free baby-sitting services for their *Shabbos* (Yiddish for Sabbath) trysting. This I now remember fondly, more fondly than my lack of studiousness under his tutelage or my transgression one Sabbath in turning on a living room light: an act forbidden as "work." As I recollect, we said some quickie prayer, asking O Lord Our God King of the Universe to burn the bulb out most immediately so that the sin might be lessened. In defiance of our sincerest importuning, the damn bulb continued to glow. Menachem Ruttenberg glowered at it, then at me and, strong man that he was, I felt a momentary fear.

This morning, however, I was just feeling annoyed at myself for feeling guilty, pissed at Judaism and Jews, and not at all responsive to my mother's contention that religion was the cure for all the anti-social habits, attitudes and dysfunctions I'd been developing. However, sensing his eyes drilling into my back, I decided to give the guy a thrill. So I began to *shokel*, sway back and forth, and pray aloud in the atonal mewling that on a good day constituted my singing voice. I closed my eyes. I got dizzy. So I put one hand to my head and shokeled and chanted more loudly. I got dizzier. A couple minutes later, I was so dizzy and trying so hard not to laugh that I began crying. I stopped only when the time came for Torah readings and rapt attention was expected, at least from those few who were still capable of faking it.

He prays with a Jewish heart . . .

I was an obnoxious child.

Among the unfairnesses of life, three affect us all, one way or another. The first is heredity. Sad to relate, we get to pick neither our genes nor those who bestow them upon us. For me, this was doubly unfortunate. My mother was the eldest daughter of two

Orthodox Jewish immigrants from what was then Austrian Galicia. Perpetual greenhorns. As the eldest, she was expected to stay home all her life, first helping with the rest of the brood – three obese sisters and an emaciated runt-of-the-litter youngest son – and then tending to her parents as they aged. This she did, and I remember her on her own death bed, down to eight-five pounds from the cancer, alternately arguing with her mother in Yiddish as to who was the favorite child and giving tearful thanks in English whenever the stout old lady, already well into her own dementia, brought her a bowl of soup or wiped her face.

It is an ugly affair to judge another human being as happy only when suffering. But such she was, and her choice of a husband at age forty guaranteed her happiness.

Leo was a violent and petty thug, about whom I never learned much and of whom no one ever spoke to me. Often unemployed and when working, engaged mostly in questionable affairs, he was observed once or twice being led away in cuffs. When not exploding, he was utterly withdrawn. In retrospect, he was clearly suffering, physically and emotionally, from his World War II Army experiences in the Aleutians and on Okinawa. Almost as clearly, in retrospect, he was given to homosexuality in its more vicious forms: a fact I came to terms with thirty years after being attacked at age thirteen by one of his friends. I'd read of the history of homosexuality among the men the Army left in the Aleutians for far too long. When I had a journalistic chance to visit the islands, I took it. While exploring some of the abandoned bunkers on Dutch Harbor, I was overcome by such a sense of evil that I nearly passed out.

It is an ugly affair to judge another human being as irredeemably malign. But sometimes, that's just the way it is.

Environment was also a problem. Thanks to my grandmother, whose squalid house we lived in, I was never hungry or homeless – that would come later – but also utterly bereft of the things everybody in that affluent neighborhood took for granted. I got an excellent public education, but I was also the kid nobody would be caught dead having lunch with. Once I decided to see how long I could go without speaking to anybody at home or in school. After three days, I finally muttered something, probably a sarcastic something, just to end the experiment.

I wasn't exactly popular. Nor should I have been. But in the final weeks of high school, when who spoke to whom no longer mattered much and status was now determined at least partially by where you were going to college, and I was going to Yale, I was finally acknowledged as some sort of human being. But it no longer mattered. I was done with it all, with the Jews I despised and with the Judaism that had been rammed down my throat as an all-purpose palliative for, and evasion of, poverty, abuse and its consequences. And that was that, except for the third and greatest of life's unfairnesses.

Character, said the Greeks, is destiny. They got that one right. Character, wrote Marcus Aurelius in his *Meditations*, requires "training and care." Practice makes perfect, even when you're practicing mistakes, in which case you perfect your mistakes. I certainly did. Whatever the particulars, in the end character is what you are and there ain't no way around it. And it is an ugly thing to realize, well into midlife, that you've lived much of your life with the character of a coward, a fool, a drunk and a bum, and no amount of socio-political exculpation or self-serving psychobabble can excuse it.

Nor can you blame it on God, if only because, just as nations get the politicians they deserve, so do people get the deities they deserve.

So what was my problem?

Simply this. I'd imploded. I was my own black hole, so imploded that nothing could escape. And so, as far as I could tell, was the God I begged, whenever I could manage to surmount the bitterness, to take away the darkness. That this God might in fact be the darkness, a darkness of our mutual creation, never occurred. An enemy, yes. An indifferent, sadistic, withholding sphincter of a God, of course. The kind of God who, to borrow from Yossl Rakover, makes it harder than it has to be, absolutely. But a god out of my own darkness? No. That's not in the Godolatrous script. God is always good.

So what does it mean to be imploded?

Simply this. Most psychologists and therapists will tell you that boundaries, clear and firm but not too rigid, are vital to human functioning and sanity. You must know what is you and where you are, and where you end and the rest of the world begins. In this sense, clinical narcissism is less about inordinate and destructive self-love (As Zeus said to Narcissus, "Watch yourself.") than about the inability to define workable boundaries: a failure usually expressed in some variant of the notion, "It's all about *me*" Or, conversely, "Nothing is ever about me." Failed boundaries can lead to sociopathic selfishness but just as easily to the paralysis of cosmic guilt and, even worse, shame. And it can lead to implosion, a condition which all the standard neuroses and dysfunctions, from depression and OCD (Obsessive-Compulsive Disorder) to inability to form relationships or relate to much of anything, are components only.

No, I wasn't living in a black hole. I'd become my own black hole, an existence in which everything, including myself, was outside me. I'd formed a character that could not escape its own implosion. And in the God of Israel, I'd found a deity to match. Only problem was, I believed in that which people call God. And I did not yet understand that only the Godolatrous faiths presume and prescribe a setting of boundaries that creates an absolute chasm between evil you and perfect deity, a chasm to be bridged only by some combination of unmerited divine generosity and imperfect yet enthusiastic human submission, whether to law or grace or inscrutable will. That humanity and deity might affect and develop each other, that it might really be a much more co-operative affair than Godolatry dared admit, and that deity itself might be rendered evil by humans, did not occur.

Of course, none of that mattered too much that fine September day in 1966 when I sat alone for the first time in my bedroom at Forty-Two Vanderbilt Hall, Old Campus, Yale University, and thought, *I'm free*. Free at last to begin to explore the world. I did. Free at last to make some good friends. I did. Free at last to tell the God of Israel to go fuck Himself and take his Chosen People along with Him to watch. I did. And I was free of it all.

Except for Israel. Somehow, Israel was different.

CHAPTER TWO

ERRAND INTO THE BEWILDEREDNESS

"For a Jewish boy, it's not a life."

So said my mother, most emphatically and in great agitation, when on or about tenth grade, I told her I was considering a free education at the Naval Academy. Just another disappointment, she indicated. First the brat refuses to do any more yeshiva summers. Then he gets himself expelled from the Hebrew Institute for something midway between sarcasm and blasphemy. Then even Menachem Ruttenberg gives up on him. Now this. Darling, where have I gone wrong?

Mom, don't get me started on that one.

The Annapolis ambition proved illusory, if only because my eyes were too bad. But a basic dilemma remained. All the teen-oriented media and even the guidance counselors said that Now Was The Time to Start Making Life Plans. True enough. But I hadn't a clue how to make a life or any other plan, nor any idea how to go about getting one. How do you get a clue when you're imploded, living in a universe not even big enough for yourself, and the God in which, despite everything you believe, is ever more conspicuous by His seeming absence? How do you un-implode?

All stop.

By this point, something should be obvious. I was imploded. Now I'm criticizing the State of Israel, the United States of America and the human race generally for being in the same collapsed/collapsing condition. Am I indulging in the Eighth Deadly Sin, cosmologizing my hang-ups?

The answer is a firm yes and no.

Erik Erikson, the brilliant lay psychoanalyst who popularized the term "identity crisis" – and who occasionally wondered whether so many people had them because they felt they were supposed to – concocted a theory, flawed but still useful, of "psycho-social epigenesis." In essence, this meant that certain positive human psychological attributes, or their opposites, developed at certain stages of life, rather like the process by which a fertilized egg becomes a future pope, terrorist or hedge fund manager. If you missed out on a certain stage, or it went awry, too bad about the dysfunction. Have an identity crisis. Erikson also studied this process in societies where conventional norms no longer either fit reality or met that society's needs: a condition guaranteed to produce identity crises *en masse*. But Erikson also considered people who solved their personal identity crises in ways that spoke to others and to the historical moment.

Moi? Maybe. Maybe not. Not for me to say. More on this, and on the theories of Erikson's younger colleague, Robert Jay Lifton, later. For now, back to the tale.

I needed some clues. I got some.

I decided to go to Yale. Why Yale? Because back then a puerile television sitcom, "The Many Loves of Dobie Gillis," featured a spoiled rich kid, Chatsworth Osborne, Jr., whose dowager mother always threatened that if he didn't shape up, he couldn't go to Yale. I figured that if Yale was good enough for Chatsworth Osborne, Jr., it was good enough for me.

I also decided to join the Marines. The impetus came from Leon Uris' best-seller, *Battle Cry*, which I read, along with *Exodus*, another paean to sanitized violence, at least a lot of times. Other, more personal and psychologically-evocative motivations doubtless contributed to this decision. But as we say in the Corps, *Semper Fi* and who gives a rodentine posterior why you joined, so long as you get with the program?

(Many years later, I came across paperback re-issues of both books. On the covers, the heroes were carrying M-16 rifles, which didn't enter service until the 1960s. *Battle Cry* was a World War II novel and *Exodus*, a tale of the founding of Israel, ended around 1950. Oh, well. Never judge a book by the rifles on its cover.)

Having charted existence through my mid-twenties, I decided to cap it off by getting a Ph.D., becoming a professor and a writer. That last, especially. Writing was the only talent I possessed; it had brought me the only recognition I'd ever received. I would apply my single great talent to some single great thing, becoming of course in the process singularly great.

So I went to Yale. I did eleven years active and reserve service in the Marines, ending up as a major, of all things. I got a Ph.D., became a prof and a journalist and author, and before leaving for Israel published a ton of stuff, most of it prescient, some of it occasionally well-received. Only problem was: I was still imploded. Only other problem was: The God of Israel was still getting His yuks at my expense. My character was proving utterly inadequate to my prospects.

So was His. And I kept having the ugly feeling that, torture-wise, He wasn't done with me yet. Nor would He be until I, like anyone in an abusive relationship, finally said, "No more" and one way or another made it stick.

Easier said than done.

My inability to extricate myself from Judaism began, not surprisingly, with sex. Senior year in high school, a new girl showed up in class. Francine was attractive and in a few years would be beautiful. She was academically brilliant, a fine pianist with a lovely voice, a skillful artist, a young woman blessed with all the talents, except the talent of making use of them, or at least of not being destroyed by them. She was troubled to the max. Her father, Abraham, a well-to-do dentist, was one of those weakling sadists who used religion to control and torment his family. Nobody was ever Jewish *enough*. When Francine, the eldest, began dating Gentile boys, her father co-opted the traumatic event as an excuse to move the family from their happy *goyische* burb to the local upscale Jewish cantonment. That's how she showed up, and we wandered into a ten-year relationship, including a five-year marriage, that never should have been.

I went to Yale. She went to Vassar. She graduated Phi Beta Kappa. I didn't. Her father declined to attend our graduations. Unavailability of sufficiently Kosher food was the proffered excuse. But no matter. Relations with Abe, whom I'd come to think of as Abie Baby, were always rocky. Still, he never pushed me too hard, lest I respond with violence (not likely) or, even worse, with something on the order of, "Yo, Abie Baby. Your daughter stays over in my room several nights a week. I've also seen her eating bacon double cheeseburgers. Which bothers you more?"

The burgers, probably.

Moral of the story: If you're determined to shrug off Judaism, marrying a Jewish woman with such a father ain't exactly the way to go about it.

And still there was Israel, land where the men all looked and acted like Paul Newman (*Exodus* was also a movie) and even the terrorists were intellectual, lovable and benign. The Six Day War was a thrill, certainly to those who watched from a safe distance. And that was the problem. I felt, deep down, that I should have been there. By 1970, my disgust with American politics and culture had reached the point where I was actively considering Aliyah, emigration. Abie Baby, an ardent Zionist, oft declaimed on the wisdom of Ben-Gurion's dictum that every American Jewish family should send one child to Israel, so as to have a personal stake in the country's survival. But when I mentioned my inclination to my soon-to-be father-in-law . . .

Not with my daughter you don't.

So back to Plan A. Leaving Abie to his collection of Israel Bonds, his newfound desire that his wife bake *challah*, bread, fresh each Friday for Shabbat, and his unaccepted offer to buy me a "Judaica library," I lied about a lifetime of allergies and asthma and took to the Corps. The initial transformation from snot-nosed Ivy League Jewish intellectual to lieutenant of Marines had its evocative moments. A nasty training accident kept me in a cast for six months and out of a tour in tail-end Vietnam. It also gave me time to ponder Christianity.

Like a lot of disaffected Jews, especially those who seek deity and who find Orthodox Judaism's nineteen zillion rules and regulations a barrier to faith – Saint Paul had a similar problem – Christianity seemed to beckon. I recall as a child sneaking down to the living room Sunday mornings to watch "Lamp unto My Feet" and similar programming. I even started a correspondence course from the Hebrew Christians of Bridgeport, lessons arriving in a plain brown envelope with no return address. They understood. My grandmother did not. She found my New Testament and study guide when most mid-adolescent males hid their *Playboys* back then: between the mattress and the box spring. Damn. Didn't know the old gal could hit that hard.

Yale offered no Christian seduction. One freshman trip to Woolsey Hall to listen to the University Chaplain, William Sloan "I'm radical; come sit at my feet" Coffin, neutered that. So did occasional encounters with the Dwight Hall do-gooders and the evangelical door-to-door God Squad. My first trip to church would have to await the Marines, and it was an awesome experience, watching every head bow in unison, every eyeball ram shut, as the command from the pulpit, "Let us pray," was intoned. I did my best to fit in, then and later. But it wasn't me. The concept of eternal salvation via a combined human sacrifice/divine suicide, as expressed across the subsequent centuries through institutionalized Godolatry, ultimately left me cold. So did original sin, vicarious atonement, strident funda-mentalism and comfy liberal social consciousness. Is that another way of saying, "Christianity's a lie"? No, not at all. It is right for those for whom it is right, true for those who accept it, and one of my most vivid memories of TV Christianity was of a Catholic priest at the end of a broadcast, staring defiantly into the camera (and at his bishop?) and reminding his audience, "Not everyone who is saved is in the Church. And not everyone who is in the Church is saved."

But if Christianity didn't permanently draw me in, neither did Judaism let me go. And from time to time, while in the Marines and experiencing occasional anti-Semitism, including one incident on a rifle range where I expected for a few seconds to be shot, I attempted to reconnect. Two incidents, the first and the last, still stand out.

I was in the Quantico Naval Hospital, recovering from surgery to piece a leg and ankle back together. I was reading the New Testament, which had just come out in the *New English Bible* edition. Prince Charles had panned the translation, so I'd asked Francine for the complete set for my birthday. On the door of my room was a note card giving my name, rank and religious "preference" (as opposed to, say, "faith" or "persuasion"). The local Jewish chaplain happened by and read my card. Then he noticed the volumes on my bed. He looked at the card again, then at me, then left without a word.

Three years later, while stationed at Camp Pendleton, I made the acquaintance of The Reb. And there ensued my final contact with Judaism for the next few decades.

"The Reb" – in Yiddish, a rabbi is called Rebbe, sometimes shortened to Reb, as in "Reb Isaac's coming to dinner" – was unmarried and uncertain whether or not he liked the Navy. The Navy, which did not always appreciate him as it should have, had stashed him with the Marines. Among other things, The Reb had pastoral responsibility for the base Women Marine company. This kept him busy. Once he was given the task of inspecting their barracks, uniforms and equipment, a "junk on the bunk" extravaganza. Together, we reviewed the "Commander's Guidance" pamphlet on what the inspecting officer should look for. How, for example, could you tell if a girdle was serviceable?

Answer: You picked it up off the bunk and tugged. I also helped The Reb conduct occasional Shabbat services.

And then there was the 1973 Passover *seder*, the dinner ritual commemorating the Israelite Exodus from Egyptian slavery.

I hadn't wanted to attend. But The Reb importuned and I didn't want him hosting yet another under-attended holiday gala. So I showed up and discovered that he'd placed me at the VIP table with the First Marine Division commander, General Adolph Schwenk; the base commander, General Herman Poggemeyer; and their ladies: two couples with even less desire to be there than I. Then, from his officiating position at the table on the dais, The Reb indicated that my task was to guide them through the complex ceremony.

Where angels fear to tread, there I galloped.

A few minutes into the seder, I noticed that the generals and their ladies were doing everything I was doing, liturgically significant or not. And so, with the assurance of a short-timer senior first lieutenant whose request for early release to attend graduate school had already been approved (separation "for the convenience of the government," the letter read), I started making up customs. "Why are we doing it this way and the chaplain's doing it another way?" they asked. "Oh," I answered casually, "that's the *Ashkenazic*, the European tradition. We're going Oriental, *Sephardic*." They nodded in agreement, looked at each other dubiously, then continued their imitations.

We came to the Ten Plagues. Normally, Plague commemoration can be effected in two ways. Either you spoon a bit of wine onto your plate as each Plague is called out, or you dip your pinky in your wine glass. I started them on pinky dips for two Plagues, then shifted them to spoonies for two more. For Plagues Five and Six, I had them banging their spoons on their plates. The Reb, who'd been watching me with skepticism, then with concern, was now turning colors, red to yellow to green to white, *seriatim*. The generals and their ladies noticed, reached the correct conclusion, glowered and glared. This persuaded me not to implement my plan for Plagues Seven through Ten: walking them around the table.

Thirty-some years later, I tracked down The Reb, who'd retired from the Navy and now had his own civilian congregation. I was applying for Aliyah. The Jewish Agency required a letter from a rabbi, certifying my Jewishness. He was the last rabbi I'd had any personal contact with. Would he please write the letter? Graciously, he did, omitting any mention of that execrable stunt and crediting me with a few *mitzvoth* I'd never performed. I sent it in. Several weeks later, I got an email from the Jewish Agency, informing me that the letter was inadequate. So I phoned.

"What's the problem?"

"He didn't say you were Jewish."

"Gila," responded I, thinking back to that rifle range incident and a few others, "being a Jewish Marine back then wasn't such fun that people were lying about it to have the experience."

"I believe. But he still didn't say directly that you're Jewish."

"What should I do?"

"Get another rabbi."

"But I don't know any other rabbis."

"Then rent one."

I did, a pleasant and engaging fellow who looked at my paperwork (mostly newspaper clippings regarding my Bar Mitzvah, first wedding, mother's burial, etc.), quizzed me on my Yiddishkeit and concluded that I was indeed Jewish. I thanked him and asked him to start talking with Erin, who was considering conversion. More on that later. But first, an apology.

Some years ago, I wrote of the Passover seder, along with some other personal misadventures regarding race relations and improper disposal of classified documents, in a magazine article. A number of Marines who'd served during the seventies got in touch to tell me, yes, that was exactly the way it was. Perhaps it was. But it was still wrong, a stupid thing to do to a pair of distinguished Marine flag officers and their wives. They're all dead now. But for what it's worth, I apologize.

I would continue doing stupid things. In 1991, they all caught up. The remnants of my universe completed their implosion. I stayed crushed for the next twenty years.

CHAPTER THREE

YOM KIPPUR PARTY GOODS

There is a considerable psychological and psychiatric literature on the faith, religion and religiosity of the deeply disturbed. I may consult it someday. But not this day. This is not to say, of course, that such studies and the therapies they generate have no value. Far from it. When you're hurting, whatever helps is helpful. I did the sit-down-and-tell-me-all-about-it therapy thing once or twice myself, with useful but transient results. I also once tried an anti-OCD drug. When the pharma kicked in, I found myself possessed of an absolutely irresistible, i.e. obsessive-compulsive, desire to do housework: a frenzy that stopped only when Erin complained that I was putting too much starch in her panty hose.

There is also a considerable theological literature on these matters. Most will tell you the obvious. God won't do for you what you ought to be doing for yourself. God will neither chew your food for you nor come across with miracles on demand. Faith does not substitute for effort. Only problem is, when the very ability to generate effort, any kind of sustained and purposeful effort, is imploded . . .

The final collapse came slowly, then quickly. Whilst living in Washington, DC, I'd gone through a disastrous second marriage, again to a Jewish woman. This time there was a child, a wonderful little boy, now a wonderful young man. After the divorce, the ex, an Alaskan, took the lad, then three years old, back to Anchorage with her. So I found myself working two jobs. I was a full-time staff writer for the now-defunct *Insight Magazine*, mostly covering national security, and a Georgetown adjunct teaching something close to a full load in two programs, plus commuting from DC to Alaska a half-dozen times a year. The loss of a child was devastating. So was the work load. So was the child support; foregoing the lawyer and signing everything put in front of me without reading was not exceptionally astute. Devastating also was the alcohol, as self-medication gradually morphed into addiction. I turned forty. I went through relationships with two good and loving women, both of whom wanted to marry. There was no way I could. Nor did I want to. Not in my perpetual emotional and, increasingly, financial disarray.

Time to regroup.

So in 1991 I asked my editor for a few weeks off to do some writing of my own. Writing in this case was an endlessly-unfinished novel I'd been schlepping around since grad school: a Washington, DC Marine Corps political thriller feminist love story. He agreed and I settled in at home to find myself do a little page-filling, a lot of drinking and some ugly pondering as to how I was getting no closer to sanity, solvency or salvation. Then one Sunday night I flicked on the tube and came across televangelist Jimmy Swaggart. Brother Jimbo's occasional moral lapses notwithstanding, he put on a pretty good show. His Biblical diction was impeccable. And I learned things from him that I wasn't likely to discover anywhere else.

That evening's sermon was from *I Samuel* 13:1-2.

"Then Nahash the Ammonite came up, and encamped against Jabesh-gilead; and all the men of Jabesh said unto Nahash, Make a covenant with us and we will serve thee. And Nahash the Ammonite answered them, On this condition will I make a covenant with you, that I may thrust out your right eyes . . ."

Now in the Gospel according to Jimbo, Nahash was a type of the Devil, and he was asking for more than surrender. Back then, Swaggart went dubiously on, men fought with their swords or spears in their right hands, their shields in their left, with only their right eyes peeking out from behind. In this imagery, to lose your right eye was to become unable to fight. To lose your ability to resist. To submit to evil, forever.

Two days later, my right eye began to feel like it had something in it. By Saturday, the pain was so intense that I dragged myself to the emergency room. The doctor took a look, then called in an ophthalmologist who told me, "You've got a badly ulcerated cornea and are in danger of losing your right eye."

I spent the final week of my write-and-regroup time-off in an orgy of eye drops, antibiotics, more eye drops, ointments, eye patchery, more eye drops, more ointments, more pain. The doctor who took over my case got the eye to heal, albeit roughly. But when I asked her repeatedly for the diagnosis, she confessed herself baffled. Finally, she concluded that I simply had one extremely dry eye, that it would always feel like I had something in it, and I would have to take care of it forever.

She may or may not have been right about the diagnosis; you never get just one dry eye. She was certainly correct about the daily/nightly drops-and-ointment routine, plus antibiotics several times a year for flare-ups . . . right until I moved to Israel, when the condition suddenly and permanently vanished.

Several months after returning to work, an exhausted little inner voice said, very quietly, *enough*.

Nineteen years later, August 2009, I was sitting at my computer in a small cottage twelve miles outside of Shelton, Washington, a town time forgot and is happy to keep on not remembering. Erin and I had been discussing Aliyah for a year or two. We'd had our application approved; all that remained was our final decision to go. For some unaccountable reason, I suddenly wanted to know the exact date of Yom Kippur, the Day of Atonement. I Googled. And on the screen appeared an ad for a party supply company. Apparently, they'd glommed onto a list of Jewish holidays, but had no idea what any of them were about. So every time a holiday approached, they ran the same basic ad.

Get Your Yom Kippur Party Goods Here.

I laughed. I called in Erin, who also laughed. The darkness began to lift, the universe to open up. No agony. No ecstasy. No thunderbolts from on-high, no Burning Bushes, no Road-to-Damascus epiphanies or Revelations in the Tower. Just . . .

Erik Erikson got it right when he wrote of identity as continuity over time and the ability of some people to resolve their crises in ways that speak to others. But he got it wrong when he under-estimated the human ability to make sudden and drastic changes. Robert Jay Lifton gave this ability a certain formulation in a controversial 1968 *Partisan Review* article, "The Protean Self," and in a later book of the same title. Proteus was the archetypal shape-shifter, a sneaky, amoral fellow at best. Lifton recast him. He deemed the Protean capability neither superficial nor hypocritical, but a key to modern survival. At some level, both men understood that resolving identity crises meant more than becoming someone in particular; it often meant becoming the person you knew you always were but couldn't quite access. To Lifton, one key lay in the ability to form "odd combinations" – to put together your own, pardon the phrasing, package, one that others might find inconsistent, offensive, even blasphemous. But what of it? If it helps, it's helpful.

Odd combinations . . .

A way of belief and of understanding belief that had already begun to come, slowly and imperfectly, to me during those hard and ugly decades of desolation . . .

Odd combinations . . .

All that reading and immersion these past two decades in the history and philosophy of late antiquity whilst watching my own self and my own country and my own world implode and keep on imploding . . .

Odd combinations . . .

Might there be some combinations, no matter how odd, that might avail here . . .

Soterion.

Once again, all stop.

Before getting into Soterion and into what I found in late antiquity, before going further into the personal, I owe the reader a simple, straightforward statement of stance concerning the role of faith, any faith, in the common world, especially the political world. From these strictures, Soterion faith is not exempt; indeed, it is especially obliged to adhere to them.

I believe that every human being has a fundamental and unalienable human right to believe or not believe in accordance with his or her persuasions, experiences and desires. Jew, Christian, Muslim, Buddhist, Hindu, Soterion, Zoroastrian, Wiccan, whatever. A human right is a precondition of human existence. Freedom of belief is such a right. Nobody needs my permission to believe. Nor am I required to give it. I am required only to respect that right, not bestow approval on how it's used.

I believe that a secular, pluralistic society, governed by a political state that has as little as possible to do with religion, is the best arrangement humankind has come up with so far. It certainly does more good for more people than the alternatives. In such a society and state, people should have the right to practice their beliefs and religion as they choose, so long as they remain reasonably within the civil law. Remaining reasonably within the civil law means, among other things: no polygamy. No slavery. No sacrifice of living beings, human or animal. No violence or intimidation. No withholding of education or medical care from the young. And if you must make a lot of noise, try to do so quietly.

In no case should religious law and stricture be enforced by the secular state. Ever.

The right to practice generates the privilege engage in certain public activities and exhibitions that have become part of the larger culture and are generally viewed as such. I've no objection to Nativity scenes in the town square or at the airport; I can extend to my fellow Americans that tolerance as a minor act of civic courtesy. I'm also willing to let the Haredi prance around outdoors all night on *Simchat Torah* and even to block off their streets to vehicular traffic on Shabbat. But I would demur at placing the Ten Instructions on the courthouse wall, if only because of the "Thou shalt have no other gods before me" number. As for those who demand such placement, you can usually shut them up or drive them to fury or both by asking them to recite the Commandments, in order. If they pass that simple test, inquire how the items relating to the Sabbath, the fear and honoring of parents, and covetousness are to be enforced.

(By the by, those who believe in the inerrancy and infallibility of the Bible can often be reduced to similar exasperation by two simple questions. Should everything forbidden in the Bible be forbidden to us? And should everything that is permitted in the Bible – slavery, concubinage, stoning witches, etc. – be permitted to us?)

I believe that religious speech should be as protected as any other form of speech, subject only to the same restrictions that apply to other speech. Rabbis, priests and ayatollahs have no more right than anyone else to shout "Fire!" in crowded theaters when there is no fire. And a lie, a deliberate misrepresentation of secular fact, remains a lie, no matter who tells it. However, religiously-based or inspired discourse merits no special consideration in the ordering of secular affairs. Rather the opposite. To explain by way of a parable:

Suppose I decide that the tree in my back yard is God. No biggie there. Lots of people have worshipped trees and sacred groves; the Hebrew goddess, Asherah, was sometimes represented by trees. Now suppose I become so enthused that I decide to share The Good News of My Tree with the world. Again, t'aint no thang. I can talk about My Tree all I want, its wisdom and miraculous powers and Master Plan for Us All, provided I don't make too great a nuisance of myself or engage in activities that are otherwise legally actionable. But the minute I walk into that school board meeting, raise my finger skyward and intone, *Thus Saith My Tree*, I've crossed a line. I am, in effect, demanding that civil society and political state heed and submit to the dictates of a supernatural entity/deity whose existence cannot be objectively proven. Nor, certainly not in the case of the Judeo-Christian deities, can there be anything resembling unanimity regarding that deity's desires and intentions. Pick an issue, any issue, and you'll usually find sincere Christians and Jews on both sides, invoking their diametrically opposed interpretations of what their allegedly common God requires.

However, even if people of faith – sometimes more aptly described as heavy users of religion – could agree, that would still constitute no mandate. To put it bluntly: God is not a citizen. Nobody's God or god or goddess or idol or tree. Not in America and not in Israel. And let's not waste time on that dreary old canard about how atheism is also a "belief system" that atheists seek to force on others. When was the last time you heard an atheist condemn you to char broil for eternity unless you saw things his way or voted for her candidate or bill? The fundamental difference is that atheists claim neither supernatural authority nor infallible knowledge of that which cannot be objectively be deemed even to exist.

Of course, people do go into the public world for all kinds of religious and spiritual reasons. This is as it should be. But they must understand that these particular motivations are not germane to the secular matters at hand. If you tell me that I should support tax cuts for the rich because you're rich and will get even richer as a result, I may not like it but you've given me an objective reason for your support. If you tell me to that you support bombing Iran because it'll bring on the End Times, and get you to Heaven faster . . . thanks, but no. And then there's the inevitable tendency of believers to conflate divine will with their own secular interests.

In sum, there's an old gag:

"How do you know you're God?"

"Well, every time I pray I find I'm talking to myself."

Not particularly funny, but those who drag their deities into secular discourse, especially political processes, need to be reminded of its implications. Your understanding of your deity may have led you to take certain stances. Fine by me. But talk to me about the secular aspects of your positions, not your spiritual reasons-why.

Don't talk about yourself. Save it for some other time and place.

I also hold to this. Since humanity first popped out of the dust or the jungle or the caves or whatever, we have plagued ourselves with two hideous evils. One has already been mentioned. Godolatry – there's only One Truth and One God and We Got It – is abhorrent. The other evil, inequality, derives much of its justification and sustenance from Godolatry. By inequality, I mean the presumption that certain persons and groups are inherently inferior to others and to be treated accordingly, i.e. used and/or oppressed by others. And nowhere does Godolatry mandate such exploitation and oppression more directly than in the matter of women. I cannot accept as humanly valid any faith that decrees women as any less than men in any way, shape or form. Women who choose voluntarily to accept that status for themselves are certainly free to do so. But I choose to shun any religious observance or situation, or religiously-inspired secular practice that mandates any kind of enforced inferior status. And let's not indulge in that old pseudo-justification, "We can be equal yet different." Agreed. But if men and women are compelled to sit separately in the synagogue or pray at The Wall, or if women may not be rabbis or priests or pastors or popes, the facts of the situation speak for themselves.

So that's a brief personal credo on the matter of where religion should fit in the world we share and the age now upon us.

Believe what you will. Let it move you as it will. But don't expect anyone else to be required to accede to it. And don't try to force it on others yourself.

Put differently: What you believe in private is your affair. When you bring it into the public world, whether through violation of the civil law or through faith-based attempts to determine what the common world should be, it becomes everybody's affair. Jesus may have said, "Judge not, lest ye be judged." But in matters pertaining to the common world, it would be more appropriate to say, "Judge constantly, and expect to be so judged." If you find yourself not liking the judgments others reach, that's your problem. And if you think you can solve your problem by violence, think twice before you start.

I am the LORD. I appeared to Abraham, Isaac, and Jacob as God Almighty, but by my name 'The LORD,' I did not make myself known to them.
Exodus 6:2-3

Jesus said,
"If you bring forth what is within you, what you bring forth will save you. If you do not bring forth what is within you, what you do not bring forth will destroy you."
The Gospel according to Thomas

CHAPTER FOUR

SOTERION

The world is filled with odd combinations, and with their progeny. Recombinance – the process by which new things, often very different from their parts, arise from combinations both unexpected and odd – drives natural as well as human history. For example, there is nothing inherent in the properties of two gases, hydrogen and oxygen, that tells you if you mix them just right, you get a liquid, water. Nor is there anything obvious in the properties of, say, Jewish religion, Hellenistic philosophy, Roman imperial government and law, and Germanic culture that tells you: mix them just right and you get Christianity. This newness is called "emergent properties" and indeed, so filled is the world with such emergence, that it's a wonder a man as brilliant as Lifton wrote as though he'd discovered the idea himself. He must have known that history is very much the story of things that weren't supposed to happen, of recombinance giving rise to events and forces that send the world off in new and different directions.

Or perhaps it's not so surprising that Lifton under-estimated the prevalence of odd combinations in human affairs. The issue, once again, is boundaries. So much of our psychological concept of self and other, of self and world, of mental health, is by historical standards, bizarre. No other civilization has ever drawn so stern a demarcation between the individual and the rest of the universe. I am me; being me separates me, so long as I live, from all else. From within myself, I may regard all else as objects fit for my manipulation, exploitation, oppression and rapine, as sources of my frustration and/or gratification. I may even experience occasional transient episodes of mystical union. But whatever my choices and interludes, I remain me and he/she/they/them/it remains other. Still, a good bit of "post-modern" psychology regards such rigidity, the "bounded, imperial self" as therapist Philip Cushman once phrased it, as itself pathological. But then, so might be the Godolatrous concept of the human relationship to divinity. You are you and will be you for all eternity, come Heaven, Hell or in-between. God is wholly other and only one possible earthly relationship exists: submission, whether to law, grace or inscrutable will. The very definition of "covenant" presumes an agreement that God offers freely and that humanity can accept or reject but not negotiate or alter.

How limited. Just as other civilizations, including those of Western antiquity, acknowledge and cherish a far greater fluidity between humankind and the natural world – boundaries far more flexible and porous – so do they cherish far more flexible and porous boundaries between humanity and divinity. And more relationships than submission are possible and desirable. Herbert Marcuse, in his scintillating yet ultimately silly attempt to reconcile Marx and Freud, did come up with one useful concept: surplus repression. Civilization requires more than a little constriction to function. But why make it harder than it has to be? Why draw the boundaries so tight? In matters of the spirit especially.

Of course, when you're just trying to stay alive, or doing mental rehearsals for ending it all, where Western civilization puts its boundaries matters less. Hunger and homelessness provide boundaries of their own and until you've dealt with those issues and their emotional aspects, the other stuff's on hold. But not entirely. Ideas and knowledge may be swirling around like dust clouds, but sometimes dust clouds display unusual emergent properties. Sometimes, out there in the cosmic void, the dust starts to swirl faster and faster, then implode, then be born again as a star. And what's true of the outer void may also be true of the inner. It just takes time.

In 1991, aged forty-three, entering on that stage of life sometimes known as maturity or "your peak earning years," I experienced a final implosion. I quit my jobs, sat in my apartment and drank until my savings ran out and I was evicted. That I survived at all is the result of encountering two people. One was a friend, a genuine Christian gentleman of the old school. The other I married.

In 1990, one on of my commutes from DC to Anchorage, I'd stopped in Seattle to interview Bruce Chapman, a former Reagan administration official and ambassador, about a think tank, Discovery Institute, that he was ramping up. I liked his approach to think tankery; the place had a pleasant feel. I wrote a favorable story on him and a year or so later, a few weeks before eviction, asked him out of the blue to affiliate me as an unpaid fellow. He did. I was now homeless and destitute, but also a senior fellow of a prestigious conservative think tank. At the time, it seemed my redemption. To simplify a complex tale, I moved to Seattle. From then until December 2002, I had an office and a title and an occasional meager income, over half of which went to child support. When I couldn't afford a small apartment or rented room, I slept in the office or *alfresco*. I also wrote books and articles and became something of a local intellectual celebrity. An interesting experience, publishing books and articles, giving speeches and doing media, then going off to spend the night wherever.

The relationship ended in 2002, when I became one of America's first mainstream conservatives to oppose, publicly and loudly, the upcoming Iraq war and the whole Bush/neocon delusion. It didn't take a lot of expertise to know what a disaster we were marching into. But Bruce was a believer. The major funders were unhappy that the Institute's senior fellow in national security affairs, a man who knew whereof he spoke, was contradicting President Bush, a gang of arrogant Jewish neocons and some over-ripe Christians for whom support of Israel meant doing their damndest to bring on Armageddon. Someone had to go. It wasn't the boss. The parting was civil.

When Discovery started out, Bruce was easily categorized: a former liberal Republican who'd morphed into a devout Reaganite. But he and, therefore, the Institute kept moving to the right and becoming more and more conservative and religiously-oriented, until they came to be seen as one of Seattle's minor embarrassments. In truth, the Institute's mix of religion and politics was becoming uncomfortably strident and embarrassing. So was its dependence on Religious Right money for its major project. By the mid-nineties, Discovery had become the *de facto* headquarters of the "Intelligent Design" (ID) movement. In theory, ID is the notion that you can seek out and study evidence of intelligent design in the natural and biological worlds without positing or inquiring into the identity, intent or even the competence of the designer. Perfectly fine in theory, except that the reality turned ID into a kind of "back-door creationism" that routinely got trashed both in the court of public opinion and in several real courts where matters such as school curricula and text selection were being adjudicated. I tried to help them clarify their tactics. "What would happen," I asked a couple of the pre-eminent IDniks, "if one day the skies opened up and a very female voice called down, 'I did it, I fucked it up, now leave me alone.'" I never did get a straight answer from those who expected their researches ultimately to yield the God of Abraham, Isaac, Jacob and Jerry (Falwell).

But it did get me thinking. If you don't have to posit divine perfection or even benign intent, you could really move some boundaries around. Those I put together with some other insights gleaned from an intense albeit non-systematic study of late antiquity and other matters, including a bit of dabble in New Age (I gave it up after attending a symposium where no one accepted that I channeled for Harry Truman). The result, after a decade or so of introspection, ponderization and multitudinous dead ends, was the framework of Soterion, and the beginnings of a vocabulary appropriate to the idea.

The word Soterion derives from the Greek *soter*, or savior. In the original usage, it denotes an earthly human, concerned primarily with earthly affairs such as military victory and just governance. An ancient king might be called a soter, with or without imputations of divinity or even divine favor. Usually, however, with. So might a soter be a "hero," a category originally reserved for the mixed progeny of deities and humans. In any case, a soter did good things in the here-and-now and showed precious little interest in what the monotheistic religions would call eternal salvation.

"Savior" derives from soter. "Messiah" derives from the Hebrew Maschiach, meaning "anointed." "Christ" derives from the Greek word for "anointed." In its original formulation, the Hebrew Maschiach was a conquering son of David, victorious in this world. The transcendent implications came later.

In Christian usage, "soteriology" is the study of salvation and salvifics. A considerable tonnage of scholarly investigation, speculation and exegesis has been devoted to this subject. Near as I can tell, little of it's worth a damn. Also in Christian usage, "soterion" is the adjectival form. It can mean, variously, "pertaining to salvation," "pertaining to one who brings salvation" or "pertaining to one who is or is about to be saved."

An odd choice of title for a way of faith that neither offers eternal you'll-always-be-you salvation nor embraces concepts such as "sin" (original or imitative), "grace" or "forgiveness." Fortunately, the term has other uses. As of this writing, on the Internet:

There's a company called Soterion Healthcare Communications that offers "Definition of Project Tasks and Resource Requirements; Project Scheduling; Content Development; Stakeholder Review Process; and Production

Management." There's also a company, Soterion LLC, touting "restorative health services," with an emphasis on "ancient medicine." There's a black metal band called Soterion. There's a for-charter, crewed luxury yacht of the same name. Soterion Studios does computer game development. There's also a lady named Kriss Soterion, a former Miss New Hampshire, now a make-up artist to various celebs and a self-described "cosmetics entrepreneur." The soterion.com site touts some fellas offering a "Christian Fantasy Role Playing World." And the soterion.org domain name belongs to the Church of Christ.

Clearly, salvation comes in many forms. But Soterion is not a guaranteed route to eternal individual salvation. It is a way of faith. In essence:

Soterion is monotheist. It posits (forgive the capitalization; Things Don't Always Become More Profound When You Capitalize Them; but it is a useful convention) a "First and Final" entity who endows creation with intelligence and purpose. This entity is not "God" as the title is commonly understood: omniscient, omnipotent, eternal, unchanging and much involved with humanity, not to say meddlesome, at all levels. Rather, Soterion monotheism tracks with Christian theologians who have long spoken of the "God behind God," the entity we can never know directly, at least not as we are. *Kabbala*, Jewish mysticism, accepts this premise. Isaac Luria, the great sixteenth century Jewish mystic, calls this First and Final, *Eyn Sof*, literally, Without Limit.

The term that finally settled on me for this First and Final was *An Cie*. But don't fret the terminologies. Just as opposing football quarterbacks can call the same play using utterly different signals, so can this First and Final be named in many ways. In Soterion, there are no names too sacred to be pronounced, or even that sacred at all.

The ancient Gnostics took this a bit farther. Gnosticism receives its name from the Greek *gnosis*, or "knowledge" – the special insight and enlightenment that comes to only a few. Once, scholars were content to shove all kinds of heresies and aberrations into this category. Over the last half century, especially since the publication of the Gnostic library discovered at Nag Hammadi, Egypt, Gnosticism has been analyzed, overanalyzed, chopped, diced, sliced and puréed. Some now claim that the term itself is valueless as a unifying category. No matter. Many Gnosticisms hold in common that the First and Final did not create the material universe. That task was performed by lesser deities emanating from the central aura. The idea is that all we can know of divinity is emanation, *aeons* or *demiurges* or whatever. This was also a staple of much Hellenistic philosophy. Kabbala asserts that the physical universe was created when Eyn Sof withdrew a part of Himself to make room, then sent in *Sefirot*, emanations, that proved too pure and powerful for mere physicality to handle, and shattered. An ID kinda god, one might say. Incompetent, although perhaps incompetent toward a greater end. In any event, Kabbala suggests that Jews pray, not to Eyn Sof, but to the Sefirot by which Eyn Sof is manifest and through which He works.

Soterion accepts that physical creation and biological life are the product of a subsidiary process. Soterion has its own names for these processes and their agents, to be discussed some other time.

Now to the fundamental difference between Soterion and the Godolatrous faiths.

Institutional monotheism presumes that divinity is an innate characteristic of the First and Final Person, Yahweh or The Father or whomever. Soterion holds that divinity is not an attribute of a First and Final at all. An Cie is beyond divinity. So are those aspects of An Cie responsible for creation. Rather, divinity is a way of faith, established for us. It's the manner in which An Cie and the creative aspects come into relationship with humanity.

Divinity, as defined here, is a *realm*, is a *passive realm*, a realm I've come to call *Khuri* and a few other things – a realm out of which human beings draw their deities, both personal and collective. Plural. Deities. Gods and goddesses and whatever else, including the evil. Such beings, and they are beings, emerge at human behest; their subsequent lives and personalities develop in co-operation or conflict with the lives and personalities of human beings. We do not make our gods and devils in our own image in some imaginary or literary or purely mythic way. We make them for real. We change and develop them; they change and develop us. Together we live and together we die or enter some other condition.

Two final basic items. First, in such manifestations, Soterion becomes "polytheist." There is no limit to the deities that may be drawn from divinity or the relationships that may develop. Nor is there any presupposition that communal and personal deities are the same. The deity of the tribe or polity may not be the same as the deity of the person. Indeed, they may be in deadly conflict. Conversely, they may be the same yet also seen and experienced quite differently. Orthodox and Gnostic Christianity tell how the risen Jesus appeared to different people in different guises. Jewish legend holds that the six hundred thousand Israelite men who stood at Sinai and heard God speak the Torah, heard six hundred thousand different Torahs. Other faiths are filled with tales of deities who appear in many different forms.

Once again, there is absolutely nothing new about this idea. What is perhaps new is the degree of the idea of co-operation and co-operative evolution between deity and humanity.

To put it simply: We've already suggested that, just as nations get the politicians they deserve, so do they get – or craft – the deities they deserve. With individuals it is no different. We're told, "Be careful what you pray for. You might get it." Perhaps it is also reasonable to suggest: "Be careful who you pray to. You might get him. Or her. Or it. Or them."

Finally, the preliminary meaning of the word "Soterion" here. If it is possible that human collectivities call forth their deities just as surely as individuals do, then perhaps we have more leeway and creativity in our relationship to collective deity than we thought. Indeed, given the confluence of crises and disasters headed our way, we may need it. A new kind of collective deity may well be useful, perhaps essential, to the survival of civilization and perhaps even the species. I've named that new kind of deity, Soterion. I suspect that, if Soterion ever forms, he or she will be an odd combination, indeed. Not a Savior in the traditional sense of bringing on the End Times or Final Judgment or whatever. Just a deity shared by enough of us to share with humanity the age and the perils now upon us.

So:

If it is true, or even plausible, that human beings are neither the passive objects of unchanging and unchangeable divine intent . . .

If their – if *our* – choices are more than the either/or of submission and adoration versus defiance and alienation . . .

If we are indeed engaged in a co-operative enterprise that changes over time . . .

If there is neither omniscience nor omnipotence nor Master Plan at work here, and things do indeed get out of hand and go wrong on both sides . . .

If there's only *us*, we humans and the deities and demons we bring forth out of our individual and collective minds and spirits . . .

Time to grow up. Our deities, both individual and communal, will be the better for it. So will we.

As to what growing up might mean specifically, what it has meant to me, as a Jew, an American and an Israeli, I don't believe it would be appropriate to delineate it here. This book is about a way of faith, not some prescribed content or my personal political and cultural agendas. And in matters of faith, few stances are more noxious, more arrogant, than "Be like me. Do as I do." Except perhaps the attitude fossilized in, "Imitate the dead."

CHAPTER FIVE

INTER-TESTAMENT

You can't say everything at once. Nor should you try to. Certainly not in a short little personal tale like this, intended more to introduce ideas and raise questions than to lay out any kind of theological system or historical meta-theory. For the present, less is more. Or at least, less is simpler.

The last chapter set forth, in very basic form, the central concepts of Soterion. They bear repeating.

Divinity, called here Khuri. Call it what you will; Soterion has no fixed dogmatic terminologies, no names too sacred to pronounce, and I've always been, well, a bit anti-semantic. Khuri, divinity, is a passive realm out of which we humans draw our deities both personal and communal. Once drawn forth, we exist and change together in a co-operative enterprise. For good and ill. The idea of a deliberately malicious "god of evil" (not the Biblical "adversary," *Ha'Satan*, an angel of God's court) is hardly new; rabbinic lore and Kabbala indeed posit that such a force is a necessary part of God's creation. That such a deity might be real and part of our own existence, growing in his or her evil as we grow in ours, is perhaps not new either. There are variants. Some Gnostics put forth the notion of a deity, evil not out of intent so much as stupidity – a subsidiary god who, unaware of his own origins, proclaimed himself the only and all-powerful One. Some stories called this deity "Samael," literally "Lord of the Blind." In at least one of the tales, Samael's boasting is ended by a stern rebuke from his mother, Sophia ("Wisdom").

No, Samael, it ain't all about you.

Might the same be said of the deity crafted by institutional Judaism and Christianity? And if so, would that conclusion be such a heresy, such a blasphemy, that those who reach it no longer have any place in Judaism or Christianity?

Perhaps. But not inevitably. The custodians and enforcers of orthodoxy certainly wouldn't like it. But just as history is often the story of things that weren't supposed to happen, so is it the story of roads not taken, of alternatives foregone, that keep coming back, whether the orthodox like it or not. The history of technology is awash to surfeit with tales of inventors and designers who were right at the wrong time. Their concept was true. But they lacked the materials, the manufacturing techniques, the computers, the financing, the market demand, to make it work. Might what is true in aircraft design also be true for faith?

Put differently: Were there people, real historical people, who were indeed right at the wrong time about deity? People to whom we should be listening now, not to resurrect them and their deities exactly as they knew them, which is impossible, but to learn from them and move on.

Yes. Most probably, yes. But you have to find them and you have to listen, and then you have to live and create on your own. We may indeed be surrounded by a cloud of witnesses. But they're witnesses only. And they won't do it for you.

Again, I cannot over-emphasize: I claim absolutely no originality, and indeed take comfort in its lack. I do not doubt that there are many people unknown to me who are writing and/or living the idea of deity as an active, evolving co-operative enterprise, not something frozen forever into Holy Writ and endless repetition of rites and ideas laid down long ago. However, not knowing them, it falls to me to proceed on my own, as best I can.

The first influence in this meandering quest, Intelligent Design, proved a trigger. Whatever ID's failure to live up to its own investigatory premise, whatever its subservience to the Religious Right, the theoretical approach is correct. Don't fret the identity, intent or competence of the designer. Just look. Be open to possibilities.

The second influence, and the third, proved far stronger. At just the right moment, I had the pleasure of discovering a singularly great book that broke down a lot of preconceptions. As for the third: A couple decades before, I'd had the honor of becoming acquainted with a truly great man whose writings opened up a world that we desperately need to understand. His legacy was there when I needed to draw upon it. Would that many more Americans someday say the same.

God: A Biography won a Pulitzer Prize and cascading praise for its author, Jack Miles, a former Jesuit priest (later an Episcopalian) and a brilliant scholar. The book's premise is simple, even if Miles did have to coin a word to describe it. Theography. The biography of God. We are taught, indeed compelled, to consider God as eternal and immutable: *I change not!* We are taught, indeed compelled, to consider God as omniscient and omnipotent. Even when we reject such characterizations, we're still crippled by lack of alternative depictions. God remains God. Miles took a different approach. He chose to treat the Hebrew Bible, which is not quite the same as the Christian Old Testament in arrangement or content, as God's biography, in which the protagonist appears, exists, acts, changes and then . . .

Disappears. Biblical scholar Richard Elliott Friedman once claimed that he may have been the first to notice this disappearance, or at least to write about it. Perhaps he was. In any case, the observation is apt. The God of *Genesis*, having created the universe, moves intimately and easily among His humans. In *Exodus*, he becomes a saving warrior and a stern lawgiver. In *Joshua* and *Judges*, He still works practical miracles. Then He slowly vanishes. The direct appearances end; the age of prophecy closes; the rabbis begin to take over, claiming for themselves the authority to explain forevermore what God desires by "interpretation" of the ancient texts. They're still at it.

Miles does not assert that God disappears, let alone dies. He does depict in detail the process by which God deteriorates into the "Ancient of Days," the old, distracted, impotent sage described in *Daniel*. He also notes that God is never even mentioned in the *Book of Esther*, and in the last historical event of the Hebrew Bible, the return of the exiles from Babylon, God and people are reunited but "nothing further is expected." And in the New Testament, God the Father is present only as invocation. The work is done by others: the Son and Holy Spirit, the human believers, the angels, and Ha'Satan, now fully Satanized, and his crew.

What's going on here?

Rabbinic lore holds that God is most powerful when most invisible, rather like that old canard about how the greatest proof of the existence of a conspiracy is the complete lack of evidence. From Masada to Auschwitz, Jews have certainly known about all-powerful deities who never seem to be around when you need them. But a more mundane reading of the Bible also avails. In Judaism, as God's direct power wanes, His demands escalate and His self-presentation via the prophets grows ever more grandiose. The greater the disasters He permits to be inflicted upon His Chosen People, the more adoration He expects. The less He gives, the more He takes, the more ardently His followers craft a legal system designed to regulate every aspect of human life, for His pleasure and in the fetishistic hope of messianic deliverance. Biblically, divine direct appearance and decisive action yield to prophecy and apocalyptics. Prophecy and apocalyptics yield to rabbinical stricture and sterility – the sterility of law piled on law and commentary piled on commentary, legend on legend, *ad infinitum*. And the rabbis, the authors and authoritarians of stricture, have run the show uninterruptedly for two thousand years. Until recently, it was they and their followers who also wrote the history. Much was twisted; much was elided. And much was left out.

So who is this God, whose biography reads like that of a man who cannot accept his own aging; who insists on blaming everybody but Himself for everything; and who demands ever more even as He delivers ever less? Who might worship – or call forth – such a deity? And who might interact with Him over time to sustain this kind of symbiosis?

"As a character," writes Miles of the early, active God, "the Lord God is disturbing as anyone is disturbing who holds immense power and seems not to know what he wants to do with it." In His relations with human beings, Miles pictures Him as a kind of play director or orchestra conductor who doesn't quite know what He wants; all He knows is that He's not getting it, and it pisses Him off. The rage is real because God's strange solitary existence makes him uniquely dependent on the humans He has created in His image:

"[God] has no social life and no private life, no life among other gods, and no self-explanatory intellectual life. He is simply not that kind of being. His only way of knowing himself seems to be through mankind as an image of himself. . . . His only way of pursuing an interest in himself is through mankind. . ."

He is, in short, a parasite. Or perhaps a parent, a violent and abusive and neglectful and megalomaniacal parent, living pathologically through His children.

Yet His obsession with His self-images also wanes, to the point where Miles can ask, "Does God Lose Interest?" He rescues His Chosen People from Egyptian bondage, then gives them a land they cannot conquer completely. The Chosen People enjoy a brief period of unity and local dominance, a status unmentioned by any record save the Bible and virtually unverified by archeological discovery. Then: disaster after disaster after disaster. Civil war and final separation. The Assyrian destruction of the Northern Kingdom of Israel, ten tribes go missing. The Babylonian conquest of the Southern Kingdom of Judea, destruction of the First Temple. Then cometh Persia. Brilliantly,

Miles sums the corpus of Hebrew prophecy during these centuries in all its frenetic confusion. It's God asking indirectly, perhaps because He cannot bear to speak the words aloud, *Can we find a way to start over?* Yes, perhaps we can. But only if humanity takes all the blame. And also, perhaps, only if humanity attributes to God a new ethical sensibility that He may or may not really hold or requite. Miles notes that, in the Jewish arrangement of the canon, God's final direct speech to a human being is the "Voice from the Whirlwind" harangue to Job. The suffering servant has questioned God's morality and justice; God replies with an extended bombast on His power. Job's final reply to God is usually presented as submission. But it's submission to power, not to justice or goodness, and Miles points out his reply may also contain more than a hint of sarcasm, deliberately omitted in translation. In any event, one conclusion is inescapable. In this arrangement of the text, Job shuts up God. Forever.

But of greatest importance here is the oft-noted fact that God claims for himself absolute unchanging unity. *Hear O Israel, the LORD Our God, the LORD Is One*. So avows the *Shema*, Judaism's most sacred prayer. But this God has different names. Orthodox commentators hold that these are titles, not names, and descriptions of various divine characteristics. Still, two titles are indisputably names. The Hebrew *Elohim*, a plural, is usually translated "God." The word LORD (as it appears capitalized in most Bibles) is the English rendering of the Tetragrammaton, YHWH, perhaps pronounced "Yahweh." "The LORD God" represents a fusion of the two. Miles develops carefully, as have many others, the perception that God and the LORD seem to have two very different personalities. God is good, or at least not out of control, even when flooding the earth. The LORD is vicious, mercurial, arbitrary, nasty. Miles holds that the Judeo-Christian God arose as a "fusion" of foreign deities whom the Israelites encountered and adopted. What if it were true literally? Not just that Elohim resembles the Canaanite El and YHWH the Canaanite Ba'al, but a literal fusion of two existing gods. Miles concludes that the fusion is inherently unstable. He does not go so far as to suggest that the fusion falls apart. Although the LORD God collapses at the end of the story, his identity holds firm. But what if it didn't?

Over time, I came to wonder whether the LORD and God had indeed come asunder. Amicable divorce? Violent expulsion of one partner? Just an irreparable drifting apart? Perhaps the LORD remained as the vicious public God of Israel, the rabbinical deity, tormenting His people across the millennia while demanding ever more by way of worship and trust. "Next year in Jerusalem," a phrase akin to "Next time it'll be different; He'll be different." Meanwhile, God, Elohim, became, in some strange quiet way, the inner God of the Jews, individually that "still, small voice" and communally a deity very different and far more humane than the imperious LORD.

He certainly became mine. The Greek word for happiness, *eudaimonia*, means literally, "a good god within." In my personal inner god, a Jewish god that I came to know as *K'el*, I found my first reconnection to Judaism. As for the outer LORD, the communal God of the Haredi and others, whom I came to know as *Kreuzias* . . . what if the two, the inner and the communal, were across the centuries in violent opposition to each other? How might that play out in human affairs and in human hearts?

An Cie. Khuri. Kreuzias. K'el. What's in a name? Not much, beyond the significance we humans attach to it. But in the act of naming anew, of shattering old categories, there can be freedom. Again, hardly an original observation. But to the extent that others have had this experience, it provides a not insignificant validation.

So I had me, at last, a sorta kinda good god within: peaceful, passive, perhaps expectant. Or perhaps merely a fragment of a former god, dispersed among at least some of His people and their descendants. A deity in divine diaspora? Perhaps. Either way, I was still a member of my people. At least, I considered myself so. But what's true for human relationships also applies to deity as a Soterion way of faith. What do you say after you say hello? And what do you do?

It took a great Stoic philosopher, also a fighter pilot who received the Medal of Honor for his leadership as a senior prisoner of war during Vietnam, to show me the way to that answer.

I first met retired Vice Admiral Jim Stockdale in 1983. I was on a postdoctoral grant in a DC think tank, writing what would become my first book. I was at my desk, flipping through the day's *Wall Street Journal*, when I came across an article by Jim, "Dignity and Honor in Vietnam." I read it through a couple times, then picked up the phone and called him out at Stanford University's Hoover Institution, where he was a senior fellow. "Hi, I'm flying out to meet you. When can you see me?" He was skeptical but agreed. I flew out to meet him. We communed on and off for a couple years. I was saddened when he became Ross Perot's 1992 running mate and humiliated himself during the vice presidential debates, and saddened more to learn that he'd been diagnosed with Alzheimer's, an exceptionally cruel end for a man of his intellect. Jim died in 2005. Since then, he has been remembered more for machismo than for wisdom. The loss is ours.

I've written about Jim Stockdale at some length in other books and articles. In this context, it's enough to report that Jim got through seven and a half years in the Hanoi Hilton by reliance on the Stoic philosophy he'd discovered as a graduate student. Stoicism, perhaps the purest of the Hellenistic "virtue ethics," provides the basis of Soterion ethics. More on that later. Jim and I never discussed Judaism or religion at all. He lived and died, near as I can tell, as something of an agnostic. But he opened to me the relevance of late antiquity, of the "inter-testamental period," to us today.

It is a fearful relevance.

As used here, the terms are deliberately imprecise and complementary. "Late antiquity," aka the "Hellenistic period," will be taken as the time from Alexander the Great's conquest of the Persian Empire, 330 BCE, to the final waning of the Roman Empire in the west in the fourth and fifth centuries CE (476 CE, the traditional death date of the Western Empire, is irrelevant here). The "inter-testamental period" begins with the final historical event of the Old Testament/Hebrew Bible, the return of the exiles from Babylon *circa* 515 BCE, the reconstituting of Judea as a province of the Persian Empire, and the building of the Second Temple. It is also likely that the Torah, the first five books of the Bible, took on its final form in Babylon and was brought back by Nehemiah or Ezra the Scribe or some such. The period ends with the canonization of the New Testament in the fourth century CE, almost a thousand years later. It is possible that the Hebrew Bible took on its canonical form around 100 CE, at a perhaps-mythical rabbinical "Council of Jamnia (Yavneh)." Everything since has been interpretation, exegesis, commentary. Nothing may be added, save by way of interpretation. Or so we are told.

Alexander's conquests, as every school person used to know, ushered in the Hellenistic Era as Greek language and culture permeated and homogenized much of the Eurasian ecumene. There appears to have been a major "die-off" of smaller cultures and their beliefs. Except, of course, for the Jews. At the same time, there began a riotous mix-and-match of Western and Oriental deities. The Greco-Roman deities were essentially state gods and goddesses; their concern was the polity. If you wanted a personal experience of such a deity, or of the deities flooding in from Persia and elsewhere, you joined a "mystery cult." Nor were you limited. You could worship and/or sample as many as you wanted.

But while the varieties of religious experience expanded and exploded, philosophy – except for the non-Hellenized Jews, the source definition of ethics and the good life, of humanity and the universe – was trending toward a conclusion. In its final centuries, much of Greco-Roman philosophy was approaching something very close to monotheism, perhaps even an ethical monotheism. Ultimately, Christianity would incorporate – some might say, steal – Stoic and other concepts of the First and Final, plus an entire supporting vocabulary. But during the preceding centuries, there was, there may have been, a fascinating encounter but between the devotees of the Hebrew God and late antiquity's groping pagan philosophers: groping toward the ethical monotheism that the Jews took as self-evident because their deity had bestowed it upon them as Law. God had offered them the Covenant of Chosenness and the Torah. One legend says that God offered it to all the other peoples of the world first; all refused. But Israel accepted and became a nation set apart. The pagan world had no such certainty, only the questings of their intellects. The Jewish apartness must have struck them as both hideous and attractive.

Still, there are many forms of apartness. During this period, the Jewish State was politically insignificant, merely a Persian, then a Greek, then a Roman province. But it had not succumbed to the die-off. Indeed, it was drawing new strength from two antithetical forces: an ever-intensifying fundamentalist, legalistic, jot-and-tittle zealotry and an ever-intensifying sophisticated cosmopolitanism. Jewish lore boasts of how the fanatical *Maccabees* successfully resisted enforced Hellenization and restored the Temple; the oil miraculously burned for eight days, etc. The legend, as celebrated annually as *Chanukah*, omits a great deal of political complexity and terroristic fratricide and is probably why the *Books of the Maccabees* are not included in the canonical Hebrew Bible. But the supposed import is clear. This little province, this tiny people, kept faith, from the Maccabean victory to the Roman disaster, when the vestiges of self-government were lost for two millennia and the people scattered among strangers who, soon enough, would turn anti-Semitism into a Christian duty, policy and recreation.

The story appeals. It also omits the facts that in Hellenistic times more Jews lived outside Judea than in it; that they were a vital part of Greco-Roman culture and intellectual life; that Judaism was an evangelical religion; and that Judaism almost brought its ethical monotheism to the world.

Almost.

Whilst researching this book, I came across a Reform Jew's paean to the past, how he felt at one with the Jews of Israel, of Auschwitz, of the ghettos of Europe, the *Marranos* (forced converts) of the Inquisition, the heroes of Masada, the Maccabees, and on and on. Utterly missing from his list were the millions of Jews who lived and created in the Hellenistic Diaspora and who – much to the delight of the rabbis and orthodox historians – vanished with little trace and less remembrance. But it is among them that I found, if indeed there is such a thing, my own ancestral home of the spirit. And I sometimes wonder. Would the Jews of the Hellenistic Diaspora have found K'el a more congenial deity than Kreuzias? And if so, was extinction their punishment, a punishment inflicted upon them by a Kreuzias who would spend the next two thousand years tormenting the people He had chosen for His own?

CHAPTER SIX

WHILE YOU WERE GONE

"You Jews. You think it's all about you."

"That's because we have a God who thinks it's all about Him."

A standard-enough exchange of views, these past two thousand years. To understand a bit about how it got to be that way, we borrow from that great American philosopher, Billy Joel. Let's go back to where the heartache began.

The history of late antiquity, of the inter-testamental era, is a tricky affair. The putative factuality of the Hebrew Bible gives me far less *tsuris* – a Yiddish word denoting heartache, heartburn and existential anxiety – than trying to sort out late antiquity. I'm perfectly willing to accept the actual physical existence of those who made the Bible stories up or wrote them down, or massaged them into a semblance of coherence, or all three. Both Testaments. I'm even willing to concede that every word is exactly what Kreuzias – how strange to use such a name – intended. Every lie. Every contradiction. Every ugliness. And also every beauty, inspiration and grace, these latter perhaps attributable to K'el (also a strange name to write), who may have had no part in the devolution into rabbinical Judaism, or perhaps who even fought it. Strange speculations. But certainly no stranger than so much of the *Talmud* (two voluminous compendia of law and commentary), Kabbala and rabbinic literature, especially that of the eighteenth-century *Hasidim*, Pietists who tried to go beyond the rabbinical establishment and ended up an establishment of their own. In any event, modern scholarship abounds with complex theories and even more complex refutations and emendations of theories on how the Hebrew Bible came to be. I cannot judge. But I've occasionally indulged a small fantasy on the subject.

It's early in King Solomon's reign and he's settling in to dazzle the world with his wisdom, establish the first Hebrew military-industrial complex and arms export industry, stock the harem, etc. Only one of David's great captains remains alive and around. Call him Jacob, a tough old warrior who never played politics, just served his king and royal friend with courage, skill and honesty. So Solomon calls him in.

"Jake, you were always faithful to my father and you never conspired against me with that no-goodnik half-brother of mine. I appreciate that. I'm going to let you live."

"I appreciate that."

"You can't stay on at court. New administration, you know. But I would like to reward you with a very nice villa and pension to match."

"I appreciate that."

"So tell me, Jake, what will you do with your time?"

"Well, Sol, er, Majesty, all those wonderful old stories we tell. I'd love to spend a few years just writing them down."

"Great idea. Creation of the universe, floods, patriarchs, matriarchs, miracles, smiting, pursuing unto, begetting, all that good stuff. Don't forget to throw in some psalms. Dad would have liked that."

"You got it."

So off goes Captain Jake, retired, to his villa. He sits down at his kitchen table and, with his wife looking over his shoulder, inscribes:

In the beginning, God created the heavens and the earth.

"That's very good, dear," says his wife. "What happens next?"

My fantasy fades when Jake, unable to proceed and growing ever more irritated with the wife's uninvited observations and suggestions, gets a job in King Solomon's think tank, the Center for Proverbial Wisdom, and in the manner of the think tanks of any millennium, produces little of value. In reality, others composed, collated, edited, revised and redacted the texts. And at some point in third century BCE, Hebrew Scriptures get translated into Greek: an event that the rabbis cursed then and have ever since. The *Septuagint*, named after the legendary seventy elders who, each working alone, allegedly produced seventy identical translations, was in many ways a lousy product. Lots of mistranslations leading to lots of misinterpretations. But apparently, there was a market for it. And not just Diaspora Jews who could no longer understand a Hebrew that had long ago fallen into everyday disuse even in Judaea. The market included Greeks.

Now, why would Greeks, i.e., Greek-speaking non-Jews want to read Jewish scripture?

Perhaps because they were looking for something, and in Judaism they almost found it. Two millennia have conditioned us to focus on what the Jews might have wanted from the Greeks, or might have resisted wanting. Perhaps it's time to consider what the Greeks might have wanted from the Jews, and what happened when they didn't get it.

We know very little about the Diaspora Jews of late antiquity. Our sources are limited for two reasons. One is physical destruction. It's mournful to realize how much more we would know, and how different our world might be, had the great library at Alexandria not burned. As for what and how much the early Christians and later on, the Muslim conquerors trashed, we'll never know. The second reason is deliberate Jewish forgetfulness. Indeed, in a sense, the Diaspora Jews of late antiquity are the real Lost Tribes. And the Orthodox would just as soon they stayed that way.

What we do know comes from a very few sources. There are three volumes by Flavius Josephus, the Jewish general who defected to the enemy during the Roman War, then spent the rest of his life cranking out justifications for his own conduct and paeans to his abandoned people's merit. There are the ample, incessant and all-but-impenetrable scribblings of Philo Judaeus, a prominent Jew of Alexandria who attempted to "reconcile" and "synthesize" Jewish scripture and law with Greek philosophy, mostly by interpreting Jewish writings allegorically, and who mercifully died before the Internet became available. There are various apocryphal and pseudo-epigraphical texts, a few nasty comments from Roman notables such as Tacitus, and more than a few *en passant* hectorings and condemnations from the rabbis in the Talmud and other literature. To this day, one of the Hebrew words for "heretic" is "Epicurean," after one of late antiquity's leading philosophies.

What we might know is this:

As the disastrous war approached, Jews comprised perhaps ten percent of the Roman Empire, about seven million souls. Perhaps half, maybe more, lived outside Judaea: in Syria, on Cyprus and especially in the great center of Hellenistic culture and thought, Alexandria, Egypt. Judaea was riven with political and religious fanaticism and corruption, seething beneath Roman occupation and chronic economic distress and inequity. Taxation was heavy; the Temple sucked inestimable wealth out of the countryside and into priestly coffers. Factions contended fiercely. There were aristocratic *Sadducees*, the Hellenizers and Roman collaborators who controlled the Temple and perhaps the royal court. They accepted the Torah but not the Oral Law that would become the written *Mishnah*, then the basis of the Talmud and the whole of Halakha. There were the Pharisees, an elite group that nonetheless "represented" the commonalty; their power bases were the synagogue and the Oral Law. There were the political extremists and terrorists, the *Sicarii*, named after the *sicarius* or dagger they carried under their robes when they went out enforcing and assassinating. Another violent outfit, the Zealots, may have formed before or during the Roman War. These groups and others took their inspiration, disastrously, from the Maccabees.

Diaspora Jews, whatever their beliefs, appear to have been relatively immune to such intense and often vicious Judaean factionalism. Perhaps they weren't even that enamored of Judaea. They refused to participate in the Roman War, whether by going there to fight or by rising up where they were. Apparently, Diaspora Jews had always paid their Temple taxes faithfully. But when Jerusalem fell under siege and the money could no longer get through, they may not have been all that heartbroken.

In short, Hellenistic Diaspora Jews were different.

In the centuries preceding the disaster of 70 CE, Diaspora Jews, especially in Alexandria, had done OK. As a group, Jews enjoyed various special privileges. Many were prosperous and influential; they participated in civic and intellectual life. Diaspora Judaism was also a religion of outreach. Throughout the Roman Empire, Gentiles became "God Fearers," regarding Judaism as a valid and compelling faith and sharing in many of its studies and rituals. But the God Fearers stopped short of full membership, refusing to take upon themselves the "Burden of the Law," especially circumcision and dietary restriction. Some perhaps were simply dabbling in Judaism; the ethos of the era encouraged such explorations. But Judaism, unlike all other options, demanded more than occasional attendance or simple obedience while in the building. Judaism demanded *conversion*, the renunciation of all other gods and practices. In practice, "Thou shalt have no other gods before me" meant no other gods, period. And the *Shema*, Judaism's creedal prayer asserts not just that God is one, but that He is God alone, the only God

And yet, it would seem, the philosophers and the thoughtful of that era, the men and women who pondered the meaning of things while the priests tended to the slaughter of animals, the pouring out of libations and the perpetual replenishment of the sacred treasury . . . it would seem that the clarifying simplicity of monotheism was exactly what they did want. A universe of intelligent design and meaning, created by a deity who cared. To repeat: In late antiquity, philosophy sometimes approached something very close to ethical monotheism, a First and Final that gave significance and purpose to human existence. Perhaps such had always been vaguely implicit in Plato's meanderings, in Aristotle's Unmoved Mover, in the *Logos* and other aspects of Stoicism. The "Hymn of Cleanthes," one of Stoicism's founders, prayed to "the God of the manifold name." But for the most part, the philosophers couldn't quite get there. For them it was always, "If such exists . . ." Judaism offered a simple, uncompromising monotheism, a clear First and Final. But to embrace the Jewish God, you also had to embrace the Jews and all their quirks and hang-ups. And it wasn't just that they didn't make it easy. It was the whole Chosen People routine. It was one thing to posture as the center of the universe in out-of-the-way Jerusalem, corrupt capital of an insignificant province and an overpriced tourist trap at that. It was quite another to do it in the midst of an advanced, sophisticated civilization that didn't much care for the conceit. Not to mention the fact that Judaism, with its emphasis on rules and regulations for everything, was the intellectual and moral antithesis of virtue ethics, which taught you how to think about what to do, but never told you what to do. And in this attraction/repulsion, perhaps, we find the origins of the world's special hatred of the Jews.

And then there was another Jewish invention, religious fanaticism. In the ancient world, religions and their deities came and went and were merged and acquired all the time. "Nothing personal, but my goddess just whupped your god. Your army has surrendered and that's that. Have a new god." Syncretism arose out of defeat and destruction as well as thought and creation. Then with the Jews, that changed. It is often assumed that the Maccabean Revolt of 168-165 BCE was occasioned by the first Gentile attempt deliberately to destroy Judaism as a faith. There is no dispute that the Seleucid ruler, Antiochus IV, did pursue a policy of forced and vicious Hellenization and desecration. Still, his motives may have been far more political than religious. One theory, based upon some Greek word play, suggests that he may simply have been nuts. But Antiochus Epiphanes, "the Divine," sometimes derided as Epimanes, "the Insane," was not a Judeophobe. Indeed, what may have incensed him was the prior refusal of the Jews to accept some of the clear benefits of Hellenization when he offered them voluntarily.

Nearly two centuries later, a genuine Roman lunatic, Caligula (ruled 37-41 CE) instigated a wave of violence against the Jews of the Diaspora, perhaps as part of his plan to institute universal emperor worship, from which the Jews previously had been exempt. Politics and madness, no doubt. But perhaps for the first time in verifiable history, the masses and the elites participated enthusiastically in the persecution. This was more than mere ethnic hatred or the explosion of various social, economic and cultural grievances. This was genuine Judeophobia, centuries before Christianity institutionalized and blessed such hatred and oppression. Why? What was it about the Jews that was beginning to arouse such uniquely virulent animosity? Perhaps the weariness and frustration with:

You Jews. You think it's all about you.

That's because we have a God who thinks it's all about Him. And you either accept the package totally or not at all.

No thanks. We want what you have. But not the way you have it. And frankly, you're not worth the hassle.

So whatever happened to the Hellenized Diaspora Jews?

The chronology of disaster is clear enough. Caligula's transient oppression killed many and established the precedent that would lead to millennia of violation, Inquisition, pogrom, genocide. It is likely that Saint Paul stripped Diaspora Judaism of the God Fearers and their political support when he declared the Jewish Law superfluous to salvation, all foods acceptable and the "true Jew" one who is "circumcised in his heart." Beginning with that success, monotheism came permanently to the Western world, but in the much simpler and easier form of Christianity. After 70 CE, the Jews were deemed, and were, a defeated and discarded sect. The Kingdom, both Kingdoms, earthly and Heavenly, had been taken away.

Also after CE 70, only one Jewish sect was left standing, the Pharisees, now operating out of the small village of Yavneh (Jamnia) and developing into the Rabbinate that would hold imploded Judaism together for the next two thousand years. Yavneh's power over the Hellenistic Diaspora is hard to assess. I suspect it was minimal: another good reason for the rabbis not to mourn their passing.

Then more disaster. About the "Kitos War" of CE 115-117 we know little, except that it comprised a series of uprisings by Diaspora Jews (in response to ample provocation?) throughout the Mediterranean basin. All were mercilessly crushed. The final act in Judea, Bar Kokhba's Rebellion, would play out to complete ruination a couple decades later. Meanwhile, Christianity was learning to hate and oppress the Jews as the people who had murdered the Savior, deicide vermin from whom nothing was any longer expected or sought.

So what finally happened to the Diaspora Jews of late antiquity? Many were murdered. Many, no doubt, became Christians and centuries later, Muslims. Others simply vanished, or survived in small enclaves throughout the Near East and the Mediterranean lands of Europe and North Africa. The first great experiment in Jewish participation in the world had ended in disaster and implosion. And the rabbis were the big winners. Just as they had been when Jerusalem fell.

Long ago, in a childhood Sunday school class that seared itself into my mind, perhaps awaiting the day I would understand, I did a workbook exercise. One of the questions: "If you had lived back then, would you rather be a Pharisee or a Sadducee?" The expected and required answer: "I would have been a Pharisee, so I could keep the laws and customs and ceremonies." After all, we were told, weren't the Sadducees the smartasses who worshipped chunks of carved marble, ran around naked in the gym and gluttonized on ham sandwiches? Who could possibly want to be like such traitors to the faith? I gave the teacher the required answer. But I also felt violated, in the manner of some one compelled to mouth words he does not believe, someone who knows that there's more to it than what they want you to know.

Forty-some years later, I realized why I'd felt that way. It wasn't just ire at the preposterous over-simplification of the controversies between the proto-Orthodox and those who valued the world that was beginning to implode around them. It was that, in the world of the Orthodox, there is room only for the Orthodox. All else must be dismissed, derided, defaced, expunged.

Still, I'd found a point of reference to reconnect to Judaism, a road not taken that appealed. Jerusalem now mattered to me less than Alexandria and the lost Temple far less than the lost library. The Hellenistic Diaspora had been a failure for lots of reasons. But it was a Judaism that faced the world and wanted to be part of the world. It may never have quite gotten out of itself. Perhaps it couldn't have. But at least it tried. Had things turned out differently . . .

Things didn't turn out differently. And that old Yiddish proverb, "Play it as it lays," always applies. As fascinating as I found Hellenistic Judaism, I was still an American Jew at the dawn of the 21st century, a Jew carrying a still-inchoate post-rabbinic sensibility and deep into alternative understandings. What, if anything, might my Soterion musings have to do with this? Under such circumstances, what might I do to begin to reconnect with my people and the ancient faith? Could it even be done at all? How far can the notion of odd combinations be stretched, especially among those who don't take kindly to unauthorized stretches?

So I did what I had to do. I got on the Net. I read. I listened. I poked around a bit. And I came away appalled. Except for the Ultra-Orthodox revival, I realized, American Judaism was dying. And given its sorry estate, there seemed to me little reason to rejoin it.

Simple demography tells the part of the tale. Of the seven billion souls on this planet, at most twenty million are Jewish. Probably closer to eighteen. Seven million-plus live in Israel, or reside elsewhere while retaining Israeli citizenship. They're relatively easy to count. Not so in America. Estimates vary from a bit over four million to maybe six and a half million, depending on self-identification and the stringency of the "Who is a Jew?" standard employed. If you take a convenient midpoint, say about five million, three hundred thousand, you find that the number of Jews in America hasn't risen in over half a century. Jews, for decades about three percent of the population, now constitute maybe two percent. Same as Muslims. Further, over half of all marriages now take place outside the faith. It would be nice to say that this often constitutes bringing people into the fold, but given the difficulty of conversion and the general Jewish indifference, there's probably a lot more going than coming.

The reasons for this decline are both many and obvious. In no particular order:

The connection to Israel no longer compels as it did when the Holocaust and the Six Day/Yom Kippur Wars were living memories for nearly all. Younger Jews especially tend to disapprove of Israel's national security policies and are put off by the Israeli counterpoint of "We're always held to a higher standard" whining and "We can do anything we please" arrogance. Liberal Jews judge Israel lacking by their own liberal standards, and the high-viz Jewish neocons, given half a chance, will nauseate nearly everyone around them.

Neither does the American Jewish establishment enjoy the clout it did. The various organizations and their leaders are case studies in self-referential atrophy; they speak primarily to, for and about themselves and their own little worlds.

Nor does the American brand selection offer much. Ultra-Orthodox "in-reach" partakes exuberantly of the shift to the fundamentalist right prevalent these last few decades in Christianity and Islam. How long the Ultra-Orthodox growth spurt might be sustained is debatable. Modern Orthodoxy gets those who still value the world and wish to practice their demanding faith in it. Meanwhile, the other recognized branches wander around in petty miasmas of their own making, preferring to call for regeneration rather than regenerate.

As for the written word: There's some fascinating and accessible scholarly research. But most non-academic Jewish writing these days, from self-help and devotional to theology, secular affairs and fiction, is dreck. And more dreck. And more dreck. The combined tonnage of trendiness and superficiality, of same old/same old and too-edgy-by-half, overwhelmed me. A previous version of this chapter, written while I was still struggling with American Judaism, named names and offered critiques. But why bother? It's their Judaism. Not mine. If it speaks to them, if it's what they need, let it be.

I could not bring myself to enter a synagogue and participate. Not out of prodigal shame, but in a total unwillingness to subject myself to that ordeal again.

Still, I could bring myself to consider Israel. In point of fact, I had no choice. My shikse wife insisted. And my shikse wife was turning out to be not so shikse after all.

The world will be freed by our liberty, enriched by our wealth, magnified by our greatness.
Theodor Herzl
The Jewish State

"Marketing agency that promoted Obama, Lance Armstrong to help Israel win over US youth."
News Item in Israeli On-line News Service YNet
27 September 2010

CHAPTER SEVEN

KASHERING THE WIFE

Am I nuts?

It was a question I could not avoid. In truth, I'd never avoided it. All my life, the answer had been, yeah, I'm nuts. But it's one thing to reach that conclusion when you're young and confident, or at least occasionally hopeful, that something's going to make it better: escape from or to some place or person, a decent job or miracle divine, a drink or a drug, a bountiful research grant or book contract. It's quite another when you're on the high side of fifty-five, unemployed and unemployable, penniless and schlepping around a private little faith you've been working on and playing with and being consumed by for well over a decade.

A faith, a way of faith, that kept changing and growing as names and ideas and prayers and little rituals got added. A way of faith I now needed and, whatever the temptation to say, *fuck it, this is nothing but dementia*, it wasn't going to go away. I was stuck with it. None of it worked. None of it mattered. Still, I would not surrender it. At least, not yet.

But I was also a Jew. So what else is new? I'd never denied it. If "Israel" really does mean "Struggles with God," then I was state-of-the-art Jewish. I was also winning. At least, it sometimes felt like I was. I'd found the essence of my return in a Judaism that vanished fifteen or more centuries ago, had been reviled by the Orthodox at the time and has been ever since – the kind of Judaism that's open to the world, openly offers what it has to the world and openly learns from the world.

Is "reviled" too strong a word? No, it's not strong enough. A thousand years after the rabbis added the "curse upon the sectarians" to the daily morning prayers, Greek philosophy re-engaged the European mind. Those Jews who got into it were given a name: perplexed. The great sage Moses Maimonides, the "Rambam," even wrote a book, *Guide of the Perplexed*, to help them get their minds right – the same Rambam who enunciated the "Thirteen Principles of Faith" that every candidate for Orthodox conversion must accept. Thirteen Principles? God only had ten. Were I a candidate for conversion today, I wouldn't get very far. I also knew enough of Jewish history to understand how seldom religious innovation and originality have ever been welcomed by the official Rabbinate. From the Haskala, the Jewish Enlightenment to the modern Reform and Reconstructionist branches, from early Hasidism to early and contemporary Zionism, change has been actively opposed and suppressed and its authors and adherents shunned and perse-cuted. Jews glory in how smart we are. But it's astonishing how so many of our most gifted people – scientists, writers, doctors, artists, musicians, statesmen – have lived and died in indif-ference or antipathy to the faith: the faith as defined by those who have been doing the defining for two thousand years. In truth, when given the chance, the vast majority of Jews get as far away from Orthodoxy as they can. They do not cease being Jews or even "authentic" Jews. They just can't tolerate the guff, or justify adherence to the obsessive-compulsive, arguably demented religiosity developed during the centuries of isolation and oppression.

And now, bro, you want to drag yourself back? What the hell for? So you can start your own branch of Judaism, get yourself excommunicated for your trouble and end up running a sect with one person in it? So you can have lots more infuriating contact with people you despise? So you can mess up what's left of your life a bit more? So you can die as crazy as you've lived?

Or maybe so that you might, with your own set of odd combi-nations and emergent properties, make some kind of contri-bution to a world that's going insane once again. Two millennia ago, Judaism was part of the world. It has yet to re-enter. Jews, yes. Israel, sorta kinda. But Judaism? No. Might I have something to contribute to that re-entry?

As that great sage, William Shatner (scion of a rabbinic family), once put it: Irony can be pretty ironic. Just as Soterion began to take on a coherent form, a form that might be personally livable and useful, America started imploding. That got in the way. But it also pointed toward something positive. And I began to wonder whether my single gift, for the written word, might be of some relevance here. Not exactly a divine mandate to go unto anybody and say anything in particular, nor to rush into the streets proclaiming The Good News of Soterion. Just a thought. A dimly held 3:00 AM kind of thought that I dared not share with anyone.

Not even my wife.

I've written that I owe my physical survival to two people. To Bruce Chapman, who gave me enough to keep me going when I was capable of doing nothing on my own behalf. And to Erin Solaro. Don't worry. This chapter will not be an extended paean to my sweetie. Few things turn people off faster than praising your mate, perhaps because so few people have, or permit themselves to have, or even acknowledge that they have, reasons for such praise. A wise old adage tells us never to criticize our mates in public; all that does is demonstrate our own poor judgment of people. The reverse, however, does not always hold. To praise your mate is not necessarily to flaunt your own acumen. Sometimes it's just to acknowledge your luck.

I first encountered Erin in 2000 on MILINET, an Internet list-serve/discussion forum for Marines and those who love them. She was beating up on a buddy of mine, a former college football star and decorated Vietnam vet, a professor at the Naval War College. I had to come to his rescue. And so I did, even while thinking that anyone who could tear my massively muscled and intellectually Ph.D'd friend up one side and down the other, then sign her riposte V/R, Very Respectfully, had to be special. I also decided to marry her. Years later, she told me that when she saw my name for the first time on an email, she also knew we'd get married.

It wasn't that simple, of course. Among the difficulties: Erin lived in Washington, DC and I was in Seattle, at the other end of the country. So we emailed and phoned for four years and decided to marry without bothering to exchange bits of trivia such as age and financial status. Then we decided to meet. In January 2004, I sent to my publisher (Carroll & Graf) the manuscript for my fifth book, *Take Back the Right: How the Neocons and the Religious Right Have Betrayed the Conservative Movement*, yet another exercise in pointless prescience. Then I hopped on Amtrak's Empire Builder, missed the connection in Chicago and four days later, looking like I'd just spent four days on a train, met my betrothed.

At the time, Erin was a thirty-something DC secretary with a useless master's degree and zero career prospects as the writer she wanted to be. Certainly, she had no future in the odd combination of fields she cared about most: national security and radical feminism. She'd been commissioned out of Indiana University ROTC as an Army lieutenant, but gave it up at the insistence of her first husband, a Marine officer. She'd worked as a professional dog trainer, specializing in animals whose behavior had brought them one step away from the pound or the euthanizing needle. She was good at redeeming the beasts, and also an avid horsewoman.

But writing was her career love. I'd read early drafts of her master's thesis for the "Diplomacy and Military Science" program at Norwich University, Vermont's well-regarded version of South Carolina's Citadel, or Virginia's VMI, the Virginia Military Institute. The thesis studied one National Guard regiment during the Buna campaign of World War II and what happened when it didn't get combat replacements. It might seem obvious. But beyond the obvious, the thesis had real-world significance, insofar as it challenged some beloved Army verities concerning troop morale and unit cohesion. It also made some devastating arguments in favor of full equality for women and gays. But it was far too ambitious academically and she wasn't getting the guidance she needed from her professors. Perhaps they ignored her because she challenged their beliefs with facts and reason; perhaps they ignored her because she was a woman. Probably both. Her board demanded so many changes that she filed her final copy with a formal addendum of protest. The University informed her that they would not bind her thesis – the imprimatur of official acceptance – until she removed the note. The thesis remains unbound. The University did not refund the binding fee.

As for radical feminism, Erin had grown up on it, agitated for the Equal Rights Amendment, volunteered in AIDS projects, and the rest. She'd also watched feminism devolve from a principled albeit tactically inept movement into an exercise in self-centered hissy-fitting. She believed that feminism, after decades of necessary concentration on individual rights and opportunities, had to return to its nineteenth century roots as the quest for full equality of responsibility for the country. She called this "civic feminism" and it made her as popular among the feminista as her thesis had endeared her to her professors.

We were clearly simpatico.

And so we settled in to decide what to do next. We'd already co-published some newspaper columns; I'd gotten her a few assignments of her own. Now it came down to:

"Look, hon, if you really want to be taken seriously as a defense writer and a feminist, you have to go to two wars to write about women soldiers and what's really going on with them. That means, Iraq to prove you can do it, Afghanistan to prove that Iraq wasn't just a fluke. All we have to do is find funding, get you accredited, get you embedded with combat troops, get you through it, find an agent, get the contract, write the book."

She agreed. And we did.

One night I got a call from Iraq. "Hi. I'm in Ramadi with the Marines. I like it here. Better than DC. I don't want to come home."

"Why don't you quit your job, sell your house and move to Seattle?"

"OK."

So she did. The book got written. *Women in the Line of Fire* was published by Seal in 2006. At first, they'd promised to make it their lead for the season. Then, for reasons never quite articulated, they refused to publicize it or even co-operate with a publicist we hired. It took a while to realize that she'd put her life on the line in two wars so that her serious study could be pushed aside in favor of books with titles like *Cunt* and *Full-Frontal Feminism*. But such was America as the wars dragged on, the economy collapsed and the citizenry staggered about in a daze of learned helplessness: passive, resentful, afraid. For half a century, America had been living on its moral and intellectual as well as its physical and monetary capital. Now it was running out. We'd moved from our condo on fashionable Mercer Island to a small cottage in the woods, to save money and to write full-time. We wanted to say things that America needed to hear. They turned out to be things that America refused to hear. The money began to run low.

And Erin confessed that her family on her mother's side had once been Jewish, and that when she agreed to move to Seattle, she also realized that someday we would make Aliyah to Israel.

Well . . . OK.

After much hesitation on my part, we began the application process. The Jewish Agency was diligent in losing our paperwork, finding it, then losing it again. When they refused to accept The Reb's letter as proof that I was Kosher, and I told them I didn't know any other rabbis, they told me to rent one. So I did, and we decided this would be an opportune moment to begin Erin's conversion process.

And that's how she learned about the broccoli.

Rabbi Harry Zeitlin was a charming man who charged us nothing. After certifying me, he turned to Erin and explained that ever since farmers stopped using DDT, harmless bacteria and other organisms had been infecting veggies. Broccoli, especially. Under the microscope, some of these looked a bit like little crustaceans, i.e., food forbidden under *Kashrut*, Jewish dietary law. Some entrepreneurial rabbis and other, scientifically-credentialed Yids were running around the country with their microscopes, offering for a fee to certify broccoli and other veggies micro-crustacean-free. Apparently, there were similar problems with New York City drinking water. We departed with this knowledge and an appointment for Erin to meet with the rabbi one-on-one the following week.

She came back from the session simultaneously irate and despondent.

"Hi, love. What did you guys talk about?"

"Broccoli."

"Anything else?"

"Mikvas."

"Ah, the ritual bath. To dip your broccoli in?"

"Don't be a Jewish brat. You people have food issues like I never imagined."

"What you mean, you people? You're tribal."

"I'm rethinking my genes."

"OK," said I, reminiscing to a prior wife. "I won't tell you what happened the time Abie Baby was reading the *Jewish Post and Opinion* and found an editorial protesting that a secular newspaper somewhere, Cincinnati maybe, had placed an article on how attendance at Jewish schools was rising next to an ad for ham. The *Post* was demanding an apology for putting the article next to, what was it that they called it? Oh, yes. The Forbidden

Item."

"You people are daft."

"You grasp of the obvious is commendable. What else?"

"I like Rabbi Zeitlin. But he wasn't exactly encouraging."

"Not after you bared your fangs?"

"I was steamed about the mikva."

"A mikva is not a steam bath. It's a pool of stagnant water."

"Another useful bit of information. What's going on here?"

"OK," said I, pouring a bourbon for me and a glass of wine for her. "Time to level."

"If you dare."

"Hey, I'm not the guy makes up the rules. But it's like this. If you're going to convert, you're expected to become a practicing, observant Jew. You can't just holler *I believe!* and that's that. Do you understand why he's reluctant?"

"I thought Israel needs people."

"They do."

"All kinds."

"It's not that simple."

"Please simplify."

I took a gulp. Nothing like Wild Turkey 101 to enhance your powers of persuasion. "In a minute. First, what's your problem with the mikva? It's the forerunner of Christian baptism, you know. You've been dunked before."

Erin took a sip. Nothing like a good Columbia Crest Washington State Merlot to enhance your powers of resistance. "Not like that. In Christianity, you do it once. Twice at the most. Jewish women have to do it all the time. Monthly, at least. It's degrading to get dunked because you're considered unclean."

"Hey, we use the mikva for more than women."

"Oh? What else?"

"Well, I believe it's also used for purifying dishes that have gotten un-Kosher."

"Jesus, you people really do have food issues. Sex issues, too.

Dirty dishes and menstruating women. That's a comfort."

Time to get metaphysical.

"Look, love, I'm sure the rabbi explained that there are lots and lots of rules that are binding only on Jews."

"Like getting dunked over and over so you can show your submission to patriarchal bearded male authority? At least dirty dishes don't have to say thank-you."

"Or leave a donation."

"You mean you have to pay for the pleasure of being humiliated by some moth-eaten rabbi who needs a bath a whole lot more than you do?"

"Steady on, love. Steady on."

"I hear men go there, too. You ever been dunked?"

"Can't say as I have. I've seen a couple mikvas, though. You know. Basement jobs in old synagogues. Smelly water. Bare swinging light bulbs overhead."

"You're not convincing me."

"I hear some of the modern ones are pretty nice. Kinda like hot tubs. Or steam baths, minus the steam. Shall I continue or would you like to jump to the meta?"

"Why don't you jump to the meta?"

"OK. The theory is this. If you become an observant Jew, your Halakhic observances add to the good in the world. But if you become Jewish and then don't practice properly, that adds to the evil. You're sinning by omission."

Erin paused a moment, then responded brightly, "But whatever I do practice, that adds to the good in the world. Right?"

"Yes," I answered, feeling the imminent need of another swallow. "But I think he suspects you'd be doing more evil than good."

"Just like most Jews. So I wouldn't be any worse than most and I might even be better than a lot."

"Point taken. Now let's explore. Judaism has six hundred and thirteen basic rules. Which would you keep?"

"The ones I can keep graciously and elegantly."

"Such as?"

"Kosher. Lots of good recipes these days. I can probably forego the pigs that God so considerately gave us to eat."

"It's about more than pigs, dear."

"I was speaking generally. Dear. Broccoli I keep regardless. What about snails?"

"Forbidden."

"That's a hard one. OK, I'll just eat them outside the house."

"Anything else you won't give up?"

"Certain sexual practices. Unless, of course, you really want me to."

"That's a hard one."

"I'll take that as a no. You could have been more emphatic."

"Where does it say in the *Shulkhan Aruch* that I have to be more emphatic?"

"What's that?"

"A one-volume compendium of all the things we need to do and avoid if we don't want to piss God off."

"I'm not afraid of God."

"The fear of the Lord is the beginning of wisdom."

"Getting over it is the advanced course."

"So why, exactly, do you want to convert? You don't need to do it to marry me. We're already married. You don't need to do it to get into Israel. As my wife, you come automatically. Then why?"

"Because," she said, sipping her wine, then smiling, "You people need me."

"Really?"

"Yes, you do. You may not know it yet, but you do. And so does your God."

"Does He know it yet?"

"Probably not."

CHAPTER EIGHT

ALIYAH

Some periods in history, the more you study them, the more you wonder: What were they thinking of? Or were they even thinking at all?

Of America since the end of the Cold War, historians may someday conclude, "Never has so much been squandered so quickly by so few." But a conclusion is not an explanation. Why did we do it? Why did we permit it to happen? Perhaps because we spent those years locked in a set of comfortable delusions, and because we'd stripped ourselves of the moral and intellectual acuity to see those delusions for what they were.

The primary delusion was "American exceptionalism" – the belief that somehow the ordinary rules don't apply to us: the belief that our civilization and our prosperity and our might were now self-perpetuating. Back in the fifties, Harvard economist John Kenneth Galbraith announced in *The Affluent Society* that the "problem of production" had been solved. All we had to do now was consume. A few years later, in *The New Industrial State*, he informed us that large-scale enterprise, that blessed combination of technology and technocracy, would keep it all going for us. Automatically. Between these two books, Robert S. McNamara, Ford executive turned secretary of defense, assured us that we could have it all, guns and butter, both galore. We were rich enough to do whatever we wanted. And by the by, there was no longer any such thing as "strategy." It all came down to "crisis management."

Thirty years later, with the Soviet Union in ruins, an obscure think tank analyst named Francis Fukuyama published an article entitled, "The End of History?" All the big problems, according to Dr. Fukuyama, had been solved. All that remained was to tend the machinery. And we were all going to be, as he put it, "bored."

Proof once again that there are some mistakes so ridiculous, only experts can make them.

In any event, by the mid-nineties, the real and long-awaited Pax Americana had arrived. We were the world's sole remaining superpower, the benevolent hegemon who would now run the world. We were good. We were strong. We were rich. We were generous and kind. We were wise. And it would go on forever.

As JFK put it, there's always some son-of-a-bitch who doesn't get the word. Osama bin Laden didn't get the word. Neither did the Chinese. And now it's fifteen years since then-Secretary of State Madeleine Albright pronounced America "the indispensable nation" and we've been learning to our sorrow just how indispensable we're not.

Or are we learning? Or are we refusing to learn because, along with the money and the power and the goodness, we've squandered our ability to think?

Had we been thinking, we might have realized that the American economy was becoming a fraud.

When you pile up scores of trillions in debt at all levels, public and private, decade after decade . . .

When you export jobs by the millions, decade after decade . . .

When you bring in foreigners by the multi-millions to take those that are left . . .

When you turn the stock market and the real estate market into fetid swamps of corruption . . .

When you permit predatory lawsuits to become a multi-billion dollar industry . . .

When you tolerate a vicious corporate health care establishment that consumes nearly twenty percent of GDP . . .

When you spend more on weapons than the rest of the world combined . . .

What did we think would happen? Or were we thinking?

And then there's the matter of war. Perpetual war, waged by a military megalith at once dominant, exorbitant and irrelevant. Who precisely we're fighting remains unclear. But had we been paying attention, we would have noticed who we're fighting *for*. With only two transient exceptions (Grenada and Panama), every significant military operation since Reagan has been undertaken at least partially *on behalf of Muslims*. From the Marines in Beirut evacuating the PLO to the Kuwaiti oil tanker reflagging; from Desert Storm to Somalia and the Balkan interventions; from the invasions and ongoing occupations of Iraq and Afghanistan to all the frenetic mucking about in Pakistan, Yemen, Africa and elsewhere. And now, as I do my final edits in April 2011, we're bombing Libya. So, *nu*? Thirty years into it, do they love us any more? Will they love us any more if we intervene in Libya or elsewhere as the Arab world continues to smolder and burn? And if Israel were to disappear tomorrow, would the *jihadi* wish us any the less defeated or dead?

And finally, there's the Dumbing Down of America, a half-century-and-counting affair that has less to do with reading Shakespeare or knowing the capitals of at least two-thirds of the states, than with a simple fact. *They want you stupid.*

They? A Conspiracy so Vast? Perhaps there is a conspiracy, and perhaps you'll find The Master Plan for the Stupefaction of America in a vault somewhere, right beside the arms of the Venus de Milo, the Holy Grail and Saddam Hussein's weapons of mass destruction. But let's not argue conspiracies. Let's just try a simple experiment. Every time you encounter some exceptionally stupid, not to say prurient or hideous, TV commercial or program or encounter corporate spin or some politician's sound bite, as ludicrous as they are arrogant, don't think, "How awful." Just remind yourself: "This is what they think of me. This is what they think I want. This is what they think I am."

And don't delude yourself that the Great American Stupefaction is simply a matter of dumbed-down school

curricula, and a cultural/media apparatus that reduces everything to entertainment and, more and more, reduces entertainment to porn. It's also physical. Alcohol, especially the prolif-
eration of cheap white liquors, especially vodka, in recent years.
Illegal drugs. Legal drugs: the mind-and-mood-altering potions
that Big Pharma markets so relentlessly and America's doctors
prescribe so compliantly. And shall we be honest? Obesity also
stupefies.

In 1937, Franklin Roosevelt declared that he saw one-third of
America ill-fed, ill-clad, ill-housed. Today we see one-third of
America over-fed, over-medicated and over-entertained. Or is it
two-thirds by now? And who benefits?

These were some of the things that Erin and I wrote about
whilst sitting in our little cottage, watching America implode.
These were some of the things that no one wanted to publish or
read. Civilization is based upon literacy. In the Beginning was
the Word. Not the image, not the sound-bite, not the spin, not the
hissy-fit, not the Tweet. But in the America of George W. Bush
and his worthy successor, Barack Obama, the Word – words of
meaning sent between citizens capable of and desirous of mutual
respect and reason – was no longer wanted. Certainly not the
words I'd been pondering about the possible relevance of a
Soterion way of faith to the American implosion.

Neither were we. And we decided that we would not die in
the streets for the sake of what America had become. But neither
would we depart until it became a matter of survival. We would
keep on writing as long as we had the money. It was a decision
we made in the full knowledge that what we were doing would
make no real-world difference, and that we would go to Israel
penniless. But it was the correct choice morally.

"This is insane," she said to me, more than once.

"More insane than what's going on?"

"Doesn't matter. Why are we rendering ourselves destitute
writing things that no one will publish? I was a soldier. I know

all about the Code of Conduct. Never surrender of your own free will while you have the means to resist. Great. But this is insane. Also pointless."

"Maybe. But if we leave, we will have shared what millions of people are going through. If we ever want to write for Americans again, maybe that provides some moral credibility."

"So whom are we leaving America to?"

"To those who are wanted there."

"Paris Hilton. Glenn Beck. Sarah Palin. Charlie Sheen. Barack Obama. Goldman, Sachs. Reality TV."

"For now."

Reluctantly, she agreed.

The money ran out. The credit dried up. A King County judge ordered me to give our, in reality Erin's, last thousand dollars to my ex, a woman then making six figures, and with our son already twenty-two. The judge, who knew full well what that payment entailed, destitution, accompanied her decision with a lecture on "responsibility" that she clearly enjoyed giving. The judge who processed our eviction simply said she was sorry. We spent our last few days in a cheap hotel, staffed by Somalis whose attitude toward us hardened appreciably when they learned where we were bound. We flew from Seattle to Philadelphia, then to Tel Aviv. When we stepped off the plane we became *olim chadashim*, new immigrants, and automatic citizens of another country that has lost its way.

Israel isn't hard to understand. The polite description is that it's part First World country, part Third World country. A less tactful but more accurate assessment would be that Israel is islands of brilliance, accomplishment, effort and tolerance, in a sea of stupidity, sloth, thuggishness, corruption and hate. The fate of Israel will be determined by whether the islands can continue to rise out of the sea, or whether the sea will flood the islands.

Put differently: The fate of Israel will be determined by how

Israelis treat each other, by what they expect and demand of each other. Israel can succumb once again to the old sinat hinam. Or it can become one of the most successful, admirable and necessary nations of the new millennium. The choice is Israel's alone. And now it was also, in some small way, ours.

Israel arose out of what Amos Oz has rightly called "a federation of visions." Theodor Herzl and several of his nineteenth century predecessors were driven by a national vision. Everybody else was getting their own country. Why not the Jews? To Herzl, a Jewish sovereign homeland would solve forever the problem of anti-Semitism; a Jewish state could be peaceful because it would have no enemies. Herzl, a cosmopolitan Austrian, wanted more than a haven. He desired a place that people would want to come to, a liberal state in the old sense of the word.

Herzl proposed. The Russians and the other East Europeans disposed. The early settlers brought their own socialist and utopian visions. The Jewish homeland would be more than a nation among nations. It would be a light unto the nations. A socialist light, with Zionist Man, strong and selfless, a new model for humanity. Then the "religious Zionists" got involved with visions of their own. What no vision reckoned with were the people already inhabiting the land and the region. A few revisionist Zionists, notably Zev Jabotinsky, understood that the Arabs would never accept the Jews and would never trade their patrimony for decent health care and a functioning bus system. They would have to be defeated and defeated until they accepted their defeat; only then would a grudging co-existence be possible. But most Zionists either ignored the existence of the Arabs or assumed that they could be bought off . . . or maybe that Jews and Arabs could gain their independence "together."

This is not the place for a disquisition on the whole sorry history of Israeli-Arab and Israeli-Palestinian relations, the tragedy and the farce and the decades of missed opportunities on all sides. But it does matter to state the obvious, if only because the obvious is so rarely made explicit.

Any Palestinian Authority or group that genuinely desires peace with Israel cannot be, as Israel currently demands, demilitarized. It must be strong enough to withstand the enmity and assaults of its radical Muslim brethren. This strengthening is going on as America (and Israel) quietly train Palestinian security forces and help create a functioning government. Over ninety percent of the West Bank is already under *de facto* Palestinian governance. But more is required. A truly independent Palestine must be at the very least an Israeli protectorate but preferably an equal Israeli ally. Could such an outlandish, impossible thing ever happen?

It may be happening now.

When Egypt wanted peace, Egypt got peace. When Jordan wanted peace, Jordan got peace. Today, Syria, the last of the "front-line" nation-state enemies, is slowly making peace. Israel is preparing for the evacuation of the Golan Heights and tending to the sundry other matters needed to implement a peace treaty.

But the old triumvirate of Egypt, Jordan and Syria has been replaced by a new set of foes: Hamas in Gaza, the Palestinian Authority (PA) on the West Bank, Hezbollah in Lebanon. These pose no threat to Israel's existence, but they can certainly do a lot of damage. Any peace with the PA would require, as a matter of PA survival, the neutralization or negation of Hezbollah and its tens of thousands of rockets aimed at Israel. Would Syria, perhaps as an unspoken part of a settlement, consent to the removal of this Iranian-backed movement and perhaps to regaining its old status as Lebanon's "protector"? What reason would they have not to? And would Lebanon, that tragic country, be better off under such an arrangement?

Would another war be necessary to achieve this? Would Syria and Israel operate together to settle with Hezbollah?

Perhaps.

With Hezbollah reduced and Hamas confined or perhaps reduced also, Israel and Palestine could begin to develop the two countries as what they are: a single economic unit.

But could it ever happen? Yes, provided there arises a generation of young Palestinians determined to end their suffering by any means necessary and give themselves and their people the nation and the life they deserve. Half a millennium ago, in the France of the religious wars, there arose a few people sometimes known as *politiques*. The politicals, determined to end the destruction. King Henry IV was born a Catholic, converted to Protestantism, then back to Catholicism. When asked about his seeming hypocrisy, he replied, "Paris is worth a Mass."

As I write, this may be happening, provided the politiques of Palestine and the rest of the Arab world can keep the Islamists and the jihadi from co-opting their revolt.

But would Israel, a state that cares less about how Arabs live than where they point their guns, abide it? Perhaps. How pleasant it would be to tell the Arab world, "Look, you guys need a couple decades, maybe more, to get yourselves together. Tend to that. Then if you still want to fight us, not to worry. We'll be here."

It could happen. Despite all the screaming about "Redemption of the Land," Israel is not an expansionist state. But those who would tie Israel's future to Bible stories represent a serious political force, one increasingly given to violence. They can be politically reduced only by an Israeli people more interested in Israel's brilliance in the world than in local boundary disputes, or in becoming just another brain-dead consumer society. Can such an Israel, at long last, come to pass?

Perhaps. The entry of a million Russians over the last twenty years has been a mixed blessing. Many brought their bad habits with them. But they also brought their genius and will to achieve; much of Israel's high-tech miracle has been wrought by them. And although many tend to be more conservative politically, many also have little patience for Bible-driven policies and Torah-based societies. What might the Russians and the secular native Israelis (of all ethnic origins) accomplish together . . . and in co-operation with several hundred thousand Jews driven out of America by economic distress and rising Judeophobia? Will the next and final Aliyah be American?

Hard to tell. But the State of Israel appears to be getting ready for it.

All in all, an interesting time to be an *oleh chadash*, a new immigrant. A new immigrant carrying a Soterion sensibility, especially, unsure what to do with it but certain that something could be done.

We arrived in late February 2010. The immigration bureaucrat at Ben-Gurion Airport pondered our papers for a while, then looked up and asked me:

"Were you ever in the Army?"

A simple question to help verify I was who I claimed to be.

"Marine Corps."

"What's that?"

I tried to explain. Twenty frustrating minutes later, after it had become abundantly apparent that no one in the office knew what the Marine Corps was, I sighed, "Yes, I was in the Army."

"I'm glad for you," she snapped.

"My wife was in the Army, too," I added helpfully.

The woman deemed the information not helpful. She got up, went to a wall safe, withdrew a wad of currency, said, "Here's your money," then waved us out of her office. We were then led outside to collect another of the benefits due new immigrants: one free taxi ride to any point in the State of Israel. An hour or so later, the cab deposited us at the Immigrant Absorption Center in Be'er-Sheva, "Gateway to the Negev." We were given the keys to our new apartment, which had been prepared for us with special treats of coffee, tea and cookies, but no electricity. So they moved us to another flat that had power, but hadn't been cleaned since the last sand storm when they'd left the windows open.

We settled in and determined to get about the business of assimilation. Erin did fine. My only problem: The hotter it got, the sicker I got. By late summer I could barely walk. My stomach was bloated and my kidneys and back were spasming painfully. So I decided to go to the doctor. Four doctors, in fact. All Russians. All women. The first, my assigned physician, was on leave. So they sent me to a second who didn't like Americans, spoke little English, wrote me a prescription for sleeping pills, then threw me out of her office. In preparation for the next doc, I wrote out a list of my ailments.

"How do you know the problem is your kidneys?" a nurse fumed irritably.

"Because my testicles are in front."

This doctor, I'd been promised, spoke English. When she adamantly denied this, I left untreated. Finally, I changed clinics and encountered a decent doc who spoke excellent English. The problem, we seemed to agree, was water. I was drinking far too much and it was wrecking my salt and electrolyte balances. Not to mention my kidneys. Just stop drinking water and everything will be fine.

"So," I concluded as I prepared to leave her office, "you're telling me that I drank American bourbon for thirty years without significant effect, but I was almost done in by Israeli bottled water."

"That is correct."

"How can I describe this in my book?"

"Just write that it's hard to be a new oleh."

I smiled. "I've been through worse."

I left the office and returned to Erin, who was preparing for her Hebrew class and cursing Eliezer Ben-Yehuda, father of modern Hebrew, in a variety of imaginative ways.

Am Yisroel Chai, thought I. No doubt about it.

The People of Israel Live.

So did I. That the ailment that I'd dismissed as so painful yet so funny, several months later might turn out to have less to do with water than with cancer, did not occur.

CHAPTER NINE

I DON'T KNOW WHERE IT IS; WHICH BUS DO I TAKE TO GET THERE?

Love lasts longer when you don't start out believing in the perfection of the beloved.

If you want to see the imperfect side of Israeli life first, begin with Be'er-Sheva, a graceless, rude and nasty midsize town that's supposed to morph into Israel's next big success story. Or so they've been saying ever since Ben-Gurion started saying it fifty, or maybe it was eighty, years ago. In truth, there's a fine university there; an excellent hospital; some secretive high-tech stuff; and *Zahal* galore (the IDF, the Israel Defense Force). But these and their upscale housing tracts exist in their own little enclaves, not to say universes. Be'er-Sheva itself needs repentance, redemption and work. At the very least, they need to clean the place up. "I shall bring you up unto a land flowing with cigarette butts, empty bottles, broken glass and plastic bags" wasn't in the original promise. Nor was the strange condition wrought by all that Gateway-to-the-Negev agriculture and urbanization. The water evaporates and remains in the air, making for perhaps the world's most humid patch of desert.

As may be clear, whilst in Be'er-Sheva I developed a profound case of Negevtivity.

The *Merkaz Klita*, the immigrant absorption center to which we'd been assigned, a huge white building, combined the least attractive aspects of late-stage public housing, unsupervised day care center and administrative ineptitude. Our flat, once we cleaned it, was more than adequate. Stepping outside was the problem. The Anglos – in America you're a Jew; when you come to Israel, you're an Anglo – were a mostly-religious potpourri, including one tall, red-bearded gent of Bible-thumping Christian origin, who'd discovered Judaism while serving in the Army in Iraq and studied for conversion in one of Saddam's old palaces. The most cultured and interesting people were the Latinos and Ukrainians. There was a clan of Yemenites who seemed determined to render themselves universally despised for their arrogance and noise, and who succeeded. The women were forbidden to speak to men, although one flouted both law and tradition when she saw me carrying an ironing board. Risking divorce, possible honor killing and certain diminution of her share of Ha'Olam Ha'Ba, she demanded that I give it to her. Since it wasn't my ironing board, I declined. The young Russians acted like young Russians. The vodka flowed, the cigarettes reeked, and it was not unusual to emerge in the morning to the comingled smells of marijuana and bacon.

Aromatics notwithstanding, Erin, who speaks some Russian, and I were starting to gain a real appreciation for them folks. Nobody, we discovered to our delight, can tell a Russian how to be a Jew. And you could get all kinds of delicacies at the gastronomes of Little Odessa. OK, so they violated both Halakha and the Law of Israel by selling the ultimate forbidden item during Passover – "Psst, hey Comrade, wanna buy some hot bread?" But there was joy in knowing that they were open on Shabbat, and one of my favorite memories is of an old gentleman, bearded and with skull cap, rushing in one Saturday afternoon, then returning to the doorway to kiss the *mezuzah* (the little prayer-containing box Jews attach to lintels). Quickly, he paid for his vodka, then ran out, then returned to slap yet another smooch on the lintel before departing, bottle clutched to his breast.

Shabbat Shalom, Tovarich. The Peace of the Sabbath be with you.

Of course, the Sabbath shut-down was not without its advantages. Among them: One day a week, you didn't have to deal with bureaucrats.

Bureaucracy here, it used to be noted, consists of an Israeli bureaucracy superimposed on a British bureaucracy, superimposed on a Turkish bureaucracy. No more. Today, Israel is fifteen percent Russian, and about ninety-eight percent of those work in government ministries. Sadly, not all of these apparatchik wannabes love Americans as they should.

Hey, guys. The Cold War's over. You lost. Deal with it.

Our adventures with Israeli bureaucracy began in America during the year or two it took the Jewish Agency to process our application, plus our eleventh-hour efforts to resolve the "You can't get your free plane ticket until you get your Aliyah visa/You can't get your Aliyah visa until you get your free plane ticket" misinformation they gave us. Be it, however, noted: The Jewish Agency has since atoned by inviting us, more than once, to join their "Tribe Thirteen Hip-Hop Initiative for New Olim," auditions in Jerusalem.

Getting our permanent ID cards took three trips to the Ministry of the Interior, including a close encounter of the worst kind with a bureaucrat who wanted to see the originals of all the documents the Jewish Agency had already lost more than once. "No," I mumbled defiantly, "you can't see the original of the rabbi's letter certifying I'm Jewish. He sent it electronically so there is no original. However, in such cases, there may be justification for regarding all copies as the original. According to the Mishnah, Tractate . . ."

Still, the Ministry of the Interior could take absurdity lessons from the Ministry of Education, whence we went to get our educations *Kashered* (the verbal form of "Kosher," as in "to Kosher" is "to Kasher"). My problem did not begin when I explained that I had no transcripts. The woman clearly understood that it was all so long ago I'd forgotten everything, so the grades really didn't matter. The problem began when she kept staring at the Latin calligraphy on my diplomas and I realized that she thought it was English. I translated calmly, and indeed remained rather tranquil until she asked me why I had a Ph.D. but no Master's. In the end, she required me to write, on the spot, a letter of explanation (apology?) to the State of Israel for showing up without an M.A.

Several months later, I was informed that the Ministry of Education, Senior Deputy Director General, Department for Evaluation of Foreign Academic Degrees, had adopted a new Ph.D. certification process, which included a personal appearance before "an experts committee." However, according to the "Application for Evaluation of Foreign Academic Degrees," to be eligible for the "appearance," the supplicant first had to present the following. I quote a partial list in the original spelling and syntax:

- Diploma of the Ph.D. degree.
- Diploma of the Bachelor and Master Degrees.
- Final official grade transcript of courses and examinations taken during the Ph.D. studies.
- Documents stating entrance examinations taken before studies for the Ph.D.
- Documents of the oral examination of the Ph.D. degree.
- Official document stating the names of the members of the examination committee, their positions within or outside the academic institution.
- Documents stating examinations (if applicable, oral and written ones) taken while the thesis research work.
- Documents stating studying years.
- Hard copy of the Ph.D. thesis.
- Official document stating the change of the name of the academic institution attended (if applicable).
- Ph.D. statement about the studies conducted towards the degree, *signed in front of a licensed Israeli lawyer*. [Italics added]
- A[n English or Hebrew] copy of the Ph.D. thesis' detailed

abstract. . . . The abstract will be forwarded to a specialist in the area of concentration of the Ph.D. research. Specialists maintain the right of asking the translation of the thesis [into Hebrew or English, if in some other language], if the abstract is not enough to reach final conclusions (translation of the methodology chapter, findings, summary and introduction part). . . .

- All documents presented to our office must be officially translated either in Hebrew or English (if the original documents are not in English or in Russian) . . . [with certification of authenticity provided by an Israeli licensed lawyer or notary].

It took me a while to understand why they were doing this. Then I realized. Terrorists by the hundreds were infiltrating Israel, posing as astrophysicists, philologists, micro-paleontologists, professors of applied abnormality and theologians from various American Baptist Bible colleges. This had to be dealt with, ruthlessly.

Opening a bank account required an hour of signing forms in Hebrew that neither of us could read. Did I sell my wife? Buy a kibbutz? Who knows? Still, the big commercial bank we chose, an institution so devoted to soaking the small customers that I expected them to charge for the privilege of taking a number and waiting your turn, had nothing on the Postal Bank. We'd been awarded a grant from a private source and had a rather large check to cash, drawn in dollars on an American bank. We'd been told that the Postal Bank charged less for currency conversion and the float time was minimal. So we made three trips to the post office to get the paperwork right, only to be told on our fourth that we couldn't deposit foreign checks until we'd had the account for one year.

"So since when does the State of Israel turn away dollars?" we asked the manager. He stared blankly and informed us, "We just learned about the rule."

We finally got our money via a discreetly recommended "check-cashing service." If you've never had the experience of standing in a back alley in Safed with a Haredi money-changer, furtively stuffing wads of two hundred shekel notes into your pockets, it's a treat. Should you ever require such services, the guy's on the Web. Tell him Erin sent you.

Grocery shopping also required acquiring new skills, derived mostly from the Israeli martial art, *Krav Maga*. Here's how you defend your cart. Here's how you grab. Here's how you cut in line at the check-out or, conversely, block out others. We also learned that Israeli store security guards, who are invariably armed, sometimes demand to check register receipts on your way out. They don't care for what or from where; they just want to see receipts. So carry some spares.

Then there was the matter of names. Every new immigrant is entitled to a Hebrew name free of charge, down at the Ministry of Interior. I poked around a bit in the dictionaries and other sources, then selected mine. Unfortunately, every time I tried to pronounce it for an Israeli, he either looked at me funny or burst out laughing. In the end, I abandoned my selection.

Probably just as well. I had no desire to go through life being known as "Lovable Submarine."

Still, the experience convinced me that the Hebrew I'd acquired forty or fifty years before might not be adequate to my present needs, especially since the only useful phrase I remembered was, "I want to go to the bathroom." Fortunately, the State of Israel thinks of everything.

When I first arrived, I was told that I would have to go into an *Ulpan*. This startled me a bit. I'd heard the word before and had naively assumed that it referred to an Israeli deep-dish pizza. But when I asked the placement worker, "Will I be going in as filling, topping or crust?" she seemed bewildered, then annoyed. Finally, she explained that an Ulpan is a total-immersion Hebrew class for new immigrants. OK, said I. So they assigned Erin to the heavy-duty class and me to a "Pensioner's Ulpan" for older adults that, I was assured, was slower than the norm, but no less rigorous.

I used to believe that "DP" stood for "Displaced Person." Now I know that it also stands for "Demented Pensioner."

My initial reaction that first class was, Good Lord, this room is full of *foreigners*. Mostly Russians, plus Hungarians, a Hungarian-speaking Canadian, Bulgarians, Latinos, a Spanish-speaking Irishman who used to tend bar in Dublin or there-abouts whilst wearing kipa, and one charming American retiree couple. The Russians dominated.

For this we won the Cold War?

The course began. The class refused to shut up. The rule is supposed to be, "Hebrew Only," but the room usually sounded like a model UN. Periodically, the teacher, a delightful and gifted young woman, would explain something. First in Russian. Then with the aid of the Canadian, in Hungarian. Then with the aid of the Irishman, in Spanish. Finally, in English. Since I was mentally, and involuntarily, recovering my old French and German, this meant that in order to understand one Hebrew word, I had to process it through at least four other languages.

Welcome to Israel.

After a month or so, the Powers-That-Be split our Ulpan in two. Those who were accomplishing nothing disappeared into a separate class. Our pace accelerated. In response to the new demands, our Russian women formed themselves into what I came to know as the "Central Committee of the Fraternal Order of Babushki." They moved all their desks together in the front of the class and, whenever one was called upon, everyone else either tried to help her or answered themselves. They rarely got much right, but at least they maintained socialist solidarity.

I stayed in the rear and concentrated on my own private technique: insanity.

When mastering a foreign language, mistakes are inevitable. Students in my Ulpan routinely said things that translated, "I sit on the air conditioner" or "I want a hairy husband." I long ago realized that I learn faster when my goofs are deliberate. So I started coming up with sentences like, "The soldier goes to the bank in his tank," "I have a cat but no sardines," "I study Hebrew because I'm in love with Tzipi Livni" and my personal fave, "How often is your birthday per kilo?"

Then I got the urge to write a political essay. In translation:

"The State of Israel has a President. His name is Shimon Peres. His job is to keep getting older. He does this very well.

"The State of Israel has a Prime Minister. His name is Bibi Netanyahu. His job is to displease everybody. He does this very well.

"The State of Israel has a Parliament. This is the *Knesset*. The Knesset has two houses. These are the Knish and the Knadle. By law, sensible legislation must originate in one house, stupid legislation in the other. Since nobody is sure which is which, this law is rarely enforced.

"The State of Israel has an Army. This is important, since Israel's philosophy of child-raising consists of a single precept. 'The Army will straighten them out.'

"The State of Israel has many ministries and bureaucracies. Their purpose is to provide jobs for Russians.

"Israel has many political parties. Nobody seems to know how many. If you can't find one you like, you start your own. Mine is the *Leumi Meshuggah*, or the "National Crazy" Party. We have no clear agenda, perhaps no agenda at all, except that anything we advocate must accord with our two basic principles. 'Why start now?' and 'Why stop now?'"

Finally, I realized that Hebrew is a rapidly evolving language, and that I could help it along. For example, the word for "Lord and Master," *Ba'al*, also means "husband" and may hark back to the ancient Canaanite god, Ba'al. After learning this, I informed the teacher that my wife doesn't do "Lord and Master" and that if I was going to be Ba'al, she had to be "Ba'al-ita." At the least. The teacher responded that there was a Hebrew word, "Ba'al-it," but it couldn't be used for "wife" and I ought to just get with the program for now. In the end, we compromised. I was Ba'al for classroom purposes. My wife was Ba'al-ita at home. And Ba'al remains in my lexicon as the Canaanite god.

Fine by me. I always wanted a hairy idol.

Unfortunately, Erin did not. She also found Hebrew extremely frustrating. At home, she expressed her ire by conceiving an intense personal hatred for Eliezer Ben-Yehuda, the obsessed and arguably obsessive early immigrant who'd single-handedly modernized Hebrew, refused to speak anything else or let his family speak anything else. She'd seen photos of Ben-Yehuda, a stiff and bearded Victorian at his cluttered desk, and concocted a somewhat disrespectful image of him. He'd be working rigidly away, making up some new word that nobody would ever be able to use or pronounce. Then he'd express his satisfaction by jumping up and doing chicken imitations, sticking his thumbs under his armpits, flapping his wings, and running around his study, making the appropriate noises. Once I realized that this animus was interfering with her academic performance, I decided to turn dismay into challenge and made up a recipe for *Marak Ben-Yehuda*, a special commemorative soup.

Marak Ben-Yehuda
Ingredients:
Twelve quarts sweet Negev rain water, preferably detoxified.
One live chicken, feathers still attached.
Two of every clean vegetable. If in doubt about a particular veggie, such as broccoli, consult rabbi or punch up halakhical-lyforbiddenveggies.org.il.
Seasonings as desired, but don't forget the horse radish.
Instructions:

Boil water.
Add chicken.
March vegetables two-by-two into pot.
Add seasonings; don't forget the horse radish.
Simmer forty days.
Remove chicken and toss from window.
If it returns with olive branch, return to pot with branch,
correct seasoning (don't forget the horse radish) and serve.
If chicken doesn't return, rejoice, then correct seasoning (forget
the horse radish) and serve anyway.

We never did get around to trying it out. But after six months, Erin could speak some pretty fair basic Hebrew. Enough to dispense with the "I don't know where it is; which bus do I take to get there?" linguistic/navigational technique. Enough to curse out people who tried to cut in line ahead of her in the grocery or on the bus. Enough to deflect all the unwelcome attention she attracted from unkempt men in the street. Enough to correct some of the more execrable behavior of the children. And enough to deal, more gently, with the religious and religion-obsessed and religion-crushed women who despised her because she was strong, proud, accustomed to freedom and unimpressed by their way of life or their reasons for adopting it.

Jews, she was learning, don't always treat each other as they should. And in Israel, rudeness is the way of life.

If he who knows not what is in the universe is a stranger to the universe, he is no less so who knows not what takes place in it.
Marcus Aurelius
Meditations

Since no one knows what will happen "in the days to come" each of us is free to fashion personal speculative visions of the future.
Emet ve Emunah
Statement of the Principles of Conservative Judaism

CHAPTER TEN

THE AGE NOW UPON US

Time to get serious again. For if Soterion as a way of faith is to have any value beyond the purely personal, it must be right for the age now upon us and the perils ahead. Soterion promises neither an End Times/Final Judgment Messiah nor an earthly embodied deliverer. It promises more: a way of faith for those who have no use for such eventualities. But to explain, first we have to name the age now upon us, at least provisionally.

There are books that few people read but lots of people know about, if only because they add some compelling idea or phrase to the lexicon. Erik Erikson did it with "identity crisis." In *The Structure of Scientific Revolutions*, Thomas Kuhn bestowed upon us "paradigm shift," a concept that has been assiduously overworked ever since. Stripped of the erudition, Kuhn's argument ran roughly:

Scientists (and people) start out with a notion of how something works, of the way things are. The earth is the center of the universe. The sun is the center of the universe. The universe has no center. The earth is flat. Whatever. Gradually, evidence begins to accumulate that it ain't necessarily so. The paradigm is adjusted to account for the new data. Over time, however, so many adjustments are required that the paradigm becomes preposterously complex and unwieldy. Then someone comes along with a new paradigm, at once simpler and more explanatory. But it doesn't triumph immediately and automatically, just because it better accords with observed and lived reality. It requires a generation to grow up with it comfortably. Then the process starts all over again.

In many ways, knowledge is cumulative. But paradigms are

always provisional. Sadly, when human beings arrange their civilizations to suit their paradigms (or ideologies), too often the provisional acquires the status of an absolute. It was true once, so it must be true now. This is unfortunate. For in human affairs, aside from death, there are only four absolutes.

Some stuff works better than others.

Everything goes wrong eventually.

Plans, as Ike used to put it, are useless; planning is essential.

And finally, the absolute contained in that wretched old Yiddish joke about the man who comes home early one afternoon and finds his wife in bed, naked, and a strange pair of men's shoes on the floor. He hears a noise in the closet, throws open the door, and there's his neighbor, shivering in his underwear and looking somewhat abashed.

"What are you doing here?" the outraged husband thunders.

His neighbor shrugs. "Everybody gotta be someplace."

And so it is with us. Everybody gotta be someplace, and this is where we are: early in the twenty-first century, residents of human and physical worlds in deep kimche, perhaps approaching catastrophic collapse. And maybe that's another absolute. In human affairs, as in nature, there is no such thing as "too big to fail." Size guarantees neither efficacy nor immortality. Rather, the reverse applies. Things get so big and complex and rigid that adaptation becomes impossible. Too many interests are involved; too many voices are heard; more often than not, change exacerbates the problems, causes new ones or both. In the end, all people can do is accept it, give up, grab for what they can and hope that the collapse doesn't come in their lifetimes. The children, despite all the "do it for the sake of the kids" pseudo-pieties, can fend for themselves.

In a sense, this book is less about absolutes than about paradigm shifts that are, or ought to be, happening. One such is a change in the concept of divinity, from active person to passive realm, and of deity from lord, judge and savior to partner . . . and friend. Now it's time to begin to consider what this might mean, how it might play out, for individuals and the species. It will require three chapters. This chapter offers a rough paradigm for the age now upon us. The next chapter deals with how a human being might make a Soterion sensibility, a Soterion way of faith, his or her own, privately. The final chapter: how to think about taking it into the common world, as Americans, as Israelis, as people who know that sometimes survival begins when you say *No!* to those who presume to tell you what your choices are. Especially when what they're offering is ultimately suicidal.

What you are about to read is the product of decades of pondering and experience: the product, also, of complex yet non-contradictory loyalties to two great nations. It is personal, not academic and certainly not "expert." It is what I've concluded. If it accords with what you know and have experienced, if it points the way to what you might be seeking and to the kind of world you think this ought to be, that's what matters. You'll find here no formal religious creed, no political or economic manifesto, no partisan polemic. But you will find an invitation to become the kind of person who, learning how to more fully inhabit his or her own life, more fully inhabits the life of nation and species, and generates some wondrous new choices thereby.

So, with that, we define the age now upon us.

The Age of the Wars of Ideology is over. Welcome to the Age of the Wars of the Ways. You may not be interested in the Wars of the Ways. But the Wars of the Ways are interested in you. In all of us. And best we start winning them. Now.

Assuming we can figure out what winning them means.

The Age of the Wars of Ideology ran roughly from the 1770s to the 1990s, from the eruption of the American Revolution to the implosion of the Soviet bloc. From Lexington and Concord and Philadelphia and Paris to Moscow and Berlin and Warsaw and Prague. The Age of the Wars of Ideology was about far more than ideology, just as the Age of the Wars of Religion of the sixteenth and seventeenth centuries was about far more than which flavor of Christianity should be the only flavor available. Still, the struggles of the eighteenth through the twentieth centuries had a leitmotif. They keyed on two great collective questions. What is the proper form of political organization for human beings? And what is the proper form of economic organization?

Francis Fukuyama wasn't entirely wrong. By the late twentieth century, it was exceedingly clear that some form of liberal political democracy with its apparatus of civil and political rights, coupled with some form of market economy/welfare state, did more good for more people than anything else yet devised. Where Fukuyama erred was in assuming that "yet devised" meant that nothing was left to think out; that all we had to do was tend the machinery and extend the benefits to the eighty or so percent of the human race that hadn't quite yet been included.

Of course, it wasn't that simple. It never is. For something both fascinating and inevitable happened during the Age of the Wars of Ideology. The questions got changed. Answering the collective questions led not just to answers but to new questions. The premise of the victorious ideologies was that the state and the economy existed for the benefit of the individual, not the other way round. The individual human being was now the standard of value. Not governments. Or corporations. Or races. Or faiths. Or clans. Or gangs. Or anything or anyone else. Nor was anyone to be deemed inferior or superior merely by virtue of membership in some group or other. The individual *qua* individual was sovereign.

But what exactly was the sovereign individual? And thus two new questions arose. What does it mean to be human? And what does it mean to be more fully human? And today these two questions dominate.

Do you doubt this? If so, then consider to what extent American politics and foreign and defense policies are affected by these concerns. Why are issues such as abortion, euthanasia and capital punishment such hot-button perennials? Why such great concern for the rights of immigrants, legal or non, and even of captured terrorists and pirates? How do these questions of humanity determine and limit how America fights?

As for Israel, a nation that has never known a moment of existence without mortal enemies on her borders and much of the world cheerfully anticipating her destruction, she wrestles with these questions in her own way. The domestic aspects of the struggle, everything from civil and economic rights for Israeli Arabs to the status of non-Jews and insufficiently Jewish Jews, are distorted by the requirement that the fight be conducted on terrain chosen by the Ultra-Orthodox and their political friends and allies. But these questions of human-ness are nonetheless compelling. And they also apply to security issues. If Israel really were an expansionist state, conducting a genocidal campaign against the Palestinians, there would have been a Palestinian "Final Solution" decades ago, and the "world community" wouldn't have done an expletive-deleted thing to stop it. Did Israel acquire nuclear weapons thirty or forty years ago? If so, then the singular fact of the Israeli arsenal has been its complete non-use. Might one expect, say, a nuclear Iran to go forty years without launching something? Perhaps inadvertently, certainly with bitterness, a famous Israeli general best captured this self-limiting concern after the Sabra and Shatila massacres of 1982, when Israeli-backed Christian militias murdered hundreds of Palestinians in Lebanon. "So Christians kill Moslems and Jews blame themselves." Yes, when they have reason to so, they do. And there are sometimes good reasons why.

When judging both the United States and Israel, the standard is not perfection. The standard is the alternative. Given the devastating power available to both nations, what might they do, what might they have done, were they not restrained by their own agonized struggles with the questions of what it means to be human and more fully human? And how much have they done these past decades, albeit so imperfectly and ineptly, to expand the answers to the questions of being human and more fully human? Suffice it to say: Even if you consider such concerns as mere fig leaves covering *Realpolitik*, or simply as self-serving lies, the very fact that these are the coverings and the lies we choose, says something important.

Most of the rest of the world is not quite so concerned.

Israel knows whom Israel fights. Israel knows whom its friends are not. The United States has no such clarity. Ever since 9/11, the country has groped for a name for the struggle. Some call it the War against Terror, as though terror were a human enemy, not a human tactic. Why not call World War II the War against Panzers or Kamikazes? Others babble about the war against "Islamo-fascism," a splendid example of the American penchant for applying Western categories to non-Western phenomena and guaranteeing thereby maximum misunderstanding. The Obama administration, in its strenuously and pathetically disingenuous 2010 white paper, *The National Security Strategy of the United States*, defined America's only enemy as "al Qaeda and its affiliates" – an evasion as ludicrous as it was transparent. At the other extreme, the military and kindred civilian types now speak tersely of "The Long War." More accurate, perhaps, but hardly more useful.

Perhaps we might define the struggle thus:

The Wars of the Ways are a myriad of conflicts, violent and non, between those nations, regions, peoples and groups who wish, in their own ways, to maintain and expand what it means to be human and more fully human and who wish to serve as guardians of the twenty-first century, against those who want out: those who prefer (as Milton put it) to rule in Hell rather than serve in Heaven. Hells of their own creation.

Who are they who would force those Hells upon us?

Islamic jihadi and religious extremists of all faiths.

Racists and ethnic separatists.

Sundry other violent types with political and cultural agendas, including eco- and animal rights terrorists.

Trans-national criminal organizations and drug cartels.

Old-fashioned political dictators and kleptocrats.

Failed and failing states, especially those with borders that make no political, economic, cultural or ethnic sense.

Male supremacists.

Thugs with agendas.

Self-empowered individuals who, for whatever reasons, seek to do harm to others, often strangers, often to as many strangers as they can.

A nasty list, and more could be adduced. But the aforementioned are only part of the problem. In the age now upon us, those who want out of the twenty-first century are increasingly allied with and draw upon those who can't get it: the billions of us who exist on a dollar or two a day, under conditions of appalling squalor, anarchy and desperation, and who may live by the motto, "When you got nothin' you got nothin' to lose." Increasingly, those who want out and those who can't get in will have access to weapons of mass destruction (nukes and enhanced conventional explosives); mass death (chemical and biological) and mass disruption (cyberwar). They can be expected to use them.

And they're networked. In the Wars of the Ways, the enemies of human and more human existence co-operate less via rigid, formal alliances than through endlessly shifting, on-again/off-again arrangements of convenience. During the Wars of Ideology, conflict and threat could be depicted by arrows on the map, and friends and allies by lines between nations. Blocs could be colored red or blue. Lists could be made. Today a more apt image might be of a net encompassing the planet, a net slowly tightening around us.

How will this all play out? That depends upon four great

human imponderables and one planetary unknown.

First, whither China? There may or may not be a Chinese Master Plan for World Domination. But they certainly seem to be following the dictum of the ancient Chinese strategist, Sun Tzu. "The greatest excellence," he wrote in *The Art of War*, "is not to win. The greatest excellence is to win without fighting." In reality, for the past several decades, China has been using barbarians to fight barbarians, i.e., letting the jihadi tie down and bankrupt the United States while lending America the money to keep on fighting and destroying itself. In reality, also, China, whatever its domestic oppressions (and they are abhorrent), has been a remarkably peaceful power. Since 1949, the country has fought only one major war, forced upon it by the United States in Korea. There have been numerous scrapes and incidents with India, Vietnam and Russia; minor territorial and boundary disputes with them and other countries; the vicious occupation of Tibet; and the ever-volatile matter of Taiwan. But China does not run around the world getting into wars. Nor does she expect to turn others into good little Chinese knock-offs. Perhaps the key to the Chinese future may lie in a simple decision to develop their own domestic economy, i.e., to raise the vast majority of their own people out of poverty. Sounds reasonable enough, and to be welcomed by all. Perhaps. Of course, a China that invests in itself would no longer need to sell to an ever-more impoverished America. Nor would such a China need to keep funding America's wars and other profligacies. It would simply arrange the planet to suit its own preferences.

What might those preferences be?

The second unknown is whether America can put its own house sufficiently in order – economically, militarily, culturally, intellectually, morally – to prosecute the Wars of the Ways effectively. This means, among other things, that the United States must get out of the business of occupying other countries in order to redeem them; that it must rebuild its morality along with its economy; and that it must abandon all notions of its own divine right to global "leadership." Nobody's following.

The third imponderable is, of course, Israel. The Zionist era is over. The nation is built. What now? At the moment, both Israel's political system and Israel's politicians are utterly inadequate to the task of crafting a post-Zionist state. The people are understandably cynical. Much will depend on how the current unrest in the Arab world plays out. But much will also depend on what kind of friendship America and Israel might develop to replace the old one. And much depends, little as Americans care to believe it, on Israel's relationship with Russia. Perhaps it's not too much to suggest that three great nations in search of new ways might come together in a manner to benefit the world.

The final imponderable: Can the young rebels of the Arab world redeem a civilization much in need of renaissance and a faith much in need of reformation? Or will they find their valor stolen and their sacrifices mere offerings on the altar of an Islamism far more vicious than they?

In sum, four imponderables that may determine who wins the Wars of the Ways. Or will it be decided by the planetary unknown? An old Klingon proverb holds, "Only a fool fights in a burning house." Or in a catastrophically changing ecosystem. Again, it is easy to imagine a confluence of crises and disasters, natural and made by humans, which threatens the very survival of the species. It would be nice to believe that humanity, having tried all the wrong answers, finally hits on the right ones. But the gravity of the collapse may be such that only divine intervention can save us.

An intervention, perhaps, at least partially of our own devising?

So what does this, any of it, have to do with the Soterion way of faith? Simply this: If the general idea appeals to you, find ways to make it work in the world. Use your intelligence, your intuition, your faith to more fully inhabit your own life as a citizen and a resident of this planet. No, you have no more right than any other person to flaunt your faith as irrefutable justification for your political and other stances and activisms. You have no more right than any other person of faith to expect others to accede to your vision. But you certainly have the same right as everyone else to claim this world as your own and to enter into the work of persuading and being persuaded, of acting and refusing to acquiesce, of finding and making your own choices, and of making them real.

Beyond suggesting that it is part of the Soterion way of faith to take up the responsibility of guardianship, I cannot tell you what your politics or social and cultural views should be. But I can tell you this: A Soterion way of faith requires that you think them through, fully and carefully, as they pertain to the age now upon us, and act upon them according to your abilities and opportunities.

Seek what finds you. The world will be the better for it. So will you.

CHAPTER ELEVEN

AN ELECTION OF DEITY

If you've made it this far, whether through genuine interest, idle curiosity, horrified fascination, or some combination thereof, I suppose it's time to get a bit coherent about what Soterion is. In essence, Soterion is a way of faith that holds that, beyond the basic postulates that divinity is passive; that we draw forth our deities, form and are formed by them; and that the proper relationship between humanity and divinity is not submission but mutual endeavor in guardianship . . . it all depends. Still, there are a few things to be said.

Maimonides, the great Jewish scholar and sage, tried to explain a lot of things, including God, by defining what they were not. Let's start there.

We – *we?* Maybe by this point there is some reason to use the plural; it certainly sounds better than another excursus into the Realm of the Vertical Pronoun. We have no canon, no sacred writings, no holy writ. We have no creed approved by committee, no authorized prayers, no doctrine. We have no concept of sin, and therefore no need of forgiveness. We pray no supplicatory prayers, nor address our deities in styles and terminologies more appropriate to Oriental despots, Mafia dons, Russian bureaucrats or American celebrities. We have no rules and regulations, no millennia of laws piled on laws, no customs and ceremonies. We leave a lot of things vague. We leave other people alone.

This is what we do have. To repeat, because it cannot be made too clear:

We have a simple concept. Divinity is the way in which aspects of the First and Final, of the Jewish Eyn Sof or my personal An Cie or whatever it might be called, come into relationship with humanity.

We have another simple concept: The realm of divinity, although perhaps actively guarded, is fundamentally passive, and that humanity draws deity out of divinity. We call forth our gods and goddesses and shape them as we will. But our gods and goddesses, once called forth, acquire wills and desires and purposes of their own. We've been doing this all along, although many have chosen not to know it, or to pretend that it's otherwise. We are responsible for our gods, individual and collective, as well as to them. That can be scary. But it's also adult.

We've yet another simple concept: Humanity and deity live and move and have their being and do things *together*. In millennia past, this "togetherness" was defined as some combination of divine initiative and human submission or rebellion. Today, it's time to grow up. More and deeper, more adult relationships are both possible and desirable. They may also be necessary.

We've yet another simple concept. A mature monotheism mandates complex deity and deities who engage us in complex ways. To envision deity as simple is as wrong as to envision deity as all-powerful or all-knowing. One of the reasons the Hellenistic philosophers never quite came to a full monotheism of the Soterion kind, was that they could never settle on what that relationship was, or even could or should be. Certainly, late antiquity held on to its civic and its patron gods and goddesses: the sacrifices and other rites designed to insure the welfare of the polity, success in war, good harvest and the rest. Whether they still believed in them is another matter. Perhaps civic worship was like standing for the national anthem. You don't have to give a damn. Perhaps nobody expects you to give a damn or cares if you give a damn. But if you don't stand up, something's amiss.

Nor did the ancients dismiss all the other polytheistic faiths as ignorant. Much of the advanced polytheism of the ancient world, from the Sumerian and Egyptian to the Hellenistic jumble, was about far more than dancing around chunks of stone or orgiastic fertility rites or child sacrifice. It was also engaged in questions of ethics and justice. In a remarkable book, *In the Wake of the Goddesses*, the late Tikva Frymer-Kensky leads us, in inexorably, to a single question: If monotheism wasn't the first ray of ethical sunlight in an otherwise dark pagan world, what was it? The answer, historically, is that it provided a definitive answer to the question of relationship. Epicureans might posit that the universe was nothing but random motion and that the gods were unaware of humanity. Stoics might conclude that the gods were aware but uninterested in or incapable of relationship. Philosophers such as Marcus Aurelius concluded more than once that, yes, the gods are aware or involved. But how? What do they want from us beyond burnt offerings and adoration? Do they even want that? Judaic monotheism answered the question by offering a concept of divine plan and history as going somewhere other than in circles, and of a deity who related history to considerations of justice and ethics as well as of power. It was all the other stuff, the tribal baggage, the ludicrous rules and regulations, the arrogance, that the ancients couldn't abide.

Which leads to yet another simple concept. All these deities of the past, did they vanish? Maybe. Maybe not. In *A Man in Full*, Tom Wolfe's novel inspired by Stoicism, he tried to resurrect Zeus a bit. The effort fell flat. But just because all those ancient deities can never be restored as they once were, nor should they be, nor can they be entreated to undertake Comeback Tours, doesn't mean they're gone forever. Humans have always wondered where they go when they die. Perhaps it's time to ask the same question of deity.

And yet another a simple concept: It's not always about us, especially those of us who pronounce ourselves a Chosen People or a band of visible saints. Nor is it always about the deity who allegedly decides that some of us are so special. Jack Miles wrote truly when he noted that the God of Israel, and by extension the

God of Christianity, has no interest or life outside of humanity. At least, that's the way the Bible, both Testaments, portrays it. In *The Religion of Israel*, Yehezkel Kaufmann, a scholar who did some of his best work in Palestine before the creation of the State of Israel, makes the point even more sternly. The Hebrew Bible knows nothing of the world beyond Israel. All else is either unimportant or merely instrumental. And one only very rarely gets a sense, in either Testament, that the rest of the world might contain some good and honest people who think about these things.

Another simple concept: Godolatry is abhorrent. It is tyrannical and vicious in itself and leads inevitably to tyranny and viciousness practiced by human beings on each other. Can one be a believing, sincere Jew or Christian without committing Godolatry? Yes. But it takes thought and courage and the ability to listen. The God of Israel, fragments of whom reside in me as perhaps in others, as such fragments of other deities do in so many of us, and might perhaps reside in all of us – this is not the same God of Israel whom the Haredi (or the Christian fundamentalists) flaunt. And it is not a matter of differing interpretations or that old evasion "God by whatever name we call Him." Mine is different. And mine is not all there is. Nor would he, nor would we, ever claim to be so.

A final simple concept: Before you can approach the realm of divinity, before you can draw forth deity, before you can form and be formed by it, you need to be . . . what? Forgiven? No. Purified? No. Born again? No. Studious? No. Meditative? No. Ecstatic? No. Initiated and certified? No. But you do need to be a certain kind of human being, or at least one who's serious about becoming such.

In the course of writing this book, I wondered many times how much of my own experiences to include: the names I'd bestowed and received; the stories I'd found; the prayers and rituals I'd developed. I finally decided to include virtually none.

At least, not yet. I've been fortunate to find and craft some lovely things. But they're my own, and neither a template for others nor a proto-orthodoxy and certainly not a new mythology, bestowed. Nor is it any part of my purpose to tell anyone what to think or do about any issue because my sense of deity commands it. As the Jews say, perish the thought. But one personal sensibility must be shared, because without it a Soterion way of faith quickly devolves into trivia, chaos or worse. Once, my character was that of a coward, a fool, a drunk, a bum. Thanks to my encounters with a great man, I was able to change sufficiently to move on to a Soterion sensibility. You may well have decided by now that Soterion faith is the greatest thing since sliced yogurt. You may have decided that I've got my head so far up my posterior, it's coming out my shoulders. But whatever your conclusions, one thing I must tell you:

Virtue ethics, especially that of Stoicism *work.*

But what are they? What makes them work?

Jim Stockdale, who once described himself as "the lawgiver of an autonomous colony of Americans who happened to be located in a Hanoi prison," was a Stoic. To survive nearly eight years in the Hanoi Hilton, he had to be. But Stoicism involves far more than graceful endurance of the soul under pressure and pain. It certainly does not require psychic numbing and implosion. The Stoic ideal was never to feel nothing. To be *apathos*, as the Greeks put it, was simply not to be jerked around by your emotions. How curious that a Greek word for "feeling" might be the root of our English word "pathological."

Jim Stockdale did his best writing on Stoicism in the seventies and eighties. Much of it appears in two anthologies put out by the Hoover Institution, *A Vietnam Experience* and *Thoughts of a Philosophical Fighter Pilot*. What makes his writing especially apt is that, at the same time he was connecting his prison experiences to the larger world and offering them to an American audience, "virtue ethics," of which Stoicism is only one form, was making an academic comeback after the better part of a century's neglect. Among its most ardent students were feminist scholars, thoughtful women pondering how women might live, now that they've attained a measure of freedom.

When professional warriors and feminist academics find the same material equally compelling, perhaps there's something going on.

In essence, there are only four types of ethical systems. Each asks a different question; each reaches a different answer. But only one is really fit for a Soterion way of faith and of life.

The first system is authoritarian, sometimes aka deontological. It posits some source of authority external to the individual and recognized by the individual as a legitimate and compelling guide to life. What does the pope say? What would Jesus do? What does the Party decree? What does the Führer require of me? How would Barack Obama or Lady Gaga handle this situation? Authority may be (to borrow from Max Weber) traditional. We do it this way because that's the way we're always done it. Authority may be legal. This is the law and that's that. Authority may be "rational." Jack's an expert. He knows what he's talking about. Best heed him. Or authority may be charismatic, adhering in the individual. I follow Judy because Judy's got *it*. In all cases, submission is the leitmotif.

The second type of system is the consequentialist, aka utilitarian. Here the standard of judgment is results: the results of your actions, the consequences of your thoughts. This type of thinking is most closely associated with philosopher Jeremy Bentham's dictum, "The greatest good of the greatest number." Poor Jeremy. Perhaps he didn't understand, or else he chose to ignore the fact that his "hedonistic calculus" reduced human beings to computers who would be condemned to validate over and over the first principle of the computer. GIGO. Garbage In. Garbage Out. You can never calculate or even know all the consequences of your actions or thoughts, and to put this principle to work in the common world is to decree that the "greatest number" is the standard of value. We're beyond such rigid tyrannies.

The third type of system is the emotivist, aka psychological. Here the fundamental question is, "How do I feel? How does this or that make me feel, especially about myself?"

If you've ever tried to live according to your feelings or, even worse, tried to live with or work for or deal with someone who does . . . enough said.

The final system is virtue ethics. Here the fundamental question is neither "What does authority say?" nor "What are the consequences?" nor "How do I feel?" The fundamental question is "How should I live? What does my life require of me?" Many answers are possible in any situation. You can certainly conclude that in any particular situation your life requires you to submit to authority, or to measure possible consequences, or to go with your gut. But in the Stoic formulation, the proper life is the life lived "according to nature." This means "the life lived according to reason." Here, English fails. Neither "nature" nor "reason" conveys the complexity of the human faculty that should govern all perceptions and decisions. Epictetus decreed it "the will" and held that all any human being truly has is his or her own will. Marcus Aurelius called it the "master faculty." In both writers, there is an additional, mystical element. Your will, your master faculty, partake in some measure of the divine aspect sometimes called *Logos*. The *Gospel according to John* begins, "In the Beginning was the Word." The Logos. In the Stoic formulation, Logos is neither a divine command nor a divine gift bestowed upon unworthy humans. It is something we share, indeed, an innate quality of the universe itself.

You share with deity the characteristic that enables deity to relate to humanity – the characteristic that lies at the essence of your own humanity and enables you to relate to divinity and deity.

But the Greeks never held that your will, your master faculty, your Logos could exist or function without training and care. Their formulations of how to train and care are complex. For our purposes, however, the whole thing rests on three simple definitions.

Virtues are human characteristics and attributes. The list of virtues is astonishingly consistent across time and space. Courage. Wisdom. Independence. Empathy. Generosity. Responsibility. Loyalty. Add your own here; finish the list. We'll most likely agree.

Values are goals, desired conditions and end states. Here there is less agreement and indeed much room for conflict. Stoicism never tells you what to want. In its pure form, it argues that everything outside your will is beyond your control and should therefore be "indifferent." However, Stoicism also holds that some "indifferents" are preferable to others. Which? It all depends on your own situation and obligations . . . for virtue ethics always affirm that, even alone on a mountain top, you have obligations and relationships to the natural world, the human world and the divine. The Stoics spoke of *cosmopolis*, literally, the city of the world, the city of the universe. They had a point.

Ethics are the rules and practices by which virtues are developed and values selected and pursued. These are contingent and subject to change.

When you put the three together, virtues, values, ethics, they sum your character. And before you approach divinity – people tend to get the deities as well as the politicians they deserve – you need to assess and understand your own character: what it is and what you want it to be.

How have you been treating your body? How have you been treating your mind? Your country? Your planet? What are your values in the world? How do you advance them? How do you handle the fact that you are part of cosmopolis? And so on. Be severe. But don't worry. An overly harsh judgment simply means that you'll get a sense of progress all the more easily, should you decide to make any changes.

But in order to make progress, you must act. What are you going to do in the age now upon us, before your fellow humans and whatever gods you may encounter or create?

When America's founders crafted and debated the Constitution, they called the process "an election of government." I suggest that before you can make an election of deity, you might make an election of character. At the very least, you'll know what you're asking your deity or deities to share.

After that, do as you and they will, for the purposes of your life together and your guardianship. And also, perhaps, for something more.

CHAPTER TWELVE

TIKKUN OLAM, TIKKUN ADON OLAM

Isaac Luria, the great sixteenth century Jewish mystic of Safed, contrived an account of the creation of the universe rather at variance with the *Genesis* version. It's always difficult to summarize Kabbala, but in essence:

When Eyn Sof decided to create a universe, His first action was *Tzimtzum*, a withdrawing of Himself to make enough space for a universe. Next came *Shevirah*. Eyn Sof sent the universe into this space as divine light held within vessels. But the vessels proved inadequate. They broke, and divine sparks were scattered everywhere. To fix the damage, to repair the universe – *Tikkun Olam* – humanity was created.

Today, Tikkun Olam, which can also be translated "repair of the world," is Judaism's chief contribution to American Political Correctness. The concept has become so conflated with left-liberal ideology that it's little more than a washed-out bromide, perhaps a joke. But the idea behind Tikkun Olam is no joke. In essence, it says that everything we do, *everything*, matters. Kabbalists embraced this concept because it linked ritual and ethics, ritual and eschatology. In Judaism (as Erin found out), keeping the commandments is presumed to add to the good in the world, whether those commandments pertain to charity, study, honesty in business, prayer or who killed the cow whose parts you're dining on. Failure to keep the commandments, whether failure of commission or omission, adds to the evil in the world.

Of course, human beings cannot fix the universe all by themselves. But in Judaism, adding to the good in the world hastens the coming of Messiah. Please note that this is the opposite of the orthodox Christian sensibility, in which Messiah came voluntarily, precisely because humanity could never do anything sufficiently worthy to bring him (An alternative Jewish idea, long-discredited but still around, is that Messiah won't come until everything is totally evil – a sin-empowering postulate that we pass over in discreet silence). Ultra-Orthodox Jews have some very definite ideas as to who and what Messiah will be and how to bring him on. Conservative Judaism leaves the matter to the individual. Reform and Reconstructionist Judaism prefer to speak of the coming of a "Messianic Age" that may or may not involve a physical Messiah, or even a Messiah as a spirit person.

If there is any plausibility to the idea that we get, individually, the deities we craft and deserve, perhaps it is also plausible that we get, collectively, the deities we craft and deserve. Now imagine with me a deity that is part-person/part moment in time. At the moment, this deity is without form and void, but might be shaped, were enough of us to offer our character and deeds, Tikkun Olam-style, to repair the world. Certainly, the world could use some fixing. Perhaps such a deity might be of relevance to the age now upon us, and the confluence of challenges and disasters coming our way.

I've come to think of such as possible deity/moment as Soterion. It's a name. And I've also gotten to wondering if, as long as we're in the business of bringing on Messiah or the Messianic Era by Tikkun Olam, perhaps we might also consider Soterion as a contribution to Tikkun Adon Olam, repair of the Lord of the Universe, our universe, in whatever forms that Lord might take.

Just a thought.

You must neither add anything to what I command you nor take anything away.
Moses' Final Charge to the People of Israel
Deuteronomy 4:2

You can't throw anything away. There is no *away*.
Ecological Maxim Also Applicable to Deity

EPILOGUE

IT'S BETTER THERE

There's an old canard about two Jews who find themselves shipwrecked on a desert island. A year later their rescuers discover that they've built three synagogues. "Well," explained one of the men. "That's the synagogue I go to. That's the synagogue he goes to. And that's the synagogue neither of us would be caught dead in."

Erin and I arrived in Be'er-Sheva in late February of 2010. By fall, we had no interest in Be'er-Sheva's multitudinous synagogues, or much of anything else about the place. We just wanted out. The physical ugliness, the rudeness and arrogance of the people, the endless petty dishonesty and cheating, the lack of any sense of vibrancy, grated on us. Now, humility and gentility are not notable Israeli qualities and in this part of the world, uncompromising honesty is not often rewarded, in business or anything else. But we wanted to be around people whose arrogance was at least based upon accomplishment, and for whom at least occasional good manners weren't regarded as signs of weakness. We were also weary of living on new immigrant allowances and studying Hebrew. We wanted to get to work, both to support ourselves and to find some kind of way to reach back to the United States.

America and Israel: two nations that have lost their way and must find it again, for their own sakes and for that of the world. We wanted to help, or at least to find a way to help. How could the nation that Israel has become talk to the nation that America is becoming? The answer is far from obvious, and despising Be'er-Sheva isn't a particularly useful way of puzzling it out.

But where to go? Tel Aviv was out of the question. Too Yuppie, too facile, too trendy, too expensive. Jerusalem, with its utterly bizarre congeries of Haredi and government people, and the hard physical ugliness of a city that has witnessed too many centuries of slaughter and is now going upscale: no way. Haifa up north seemed promising. There was civilization and civility, and a university perhaps just open enough to have us. And people were telling us, "Go North." It's better there. Not just Haifa but much of the Galilee. It's physically spectacular. The people are nicer and more interesting. There are possibilities.

I was too sick to travel. So in November, Erin went up alone to spy out the land. She came back with a good report. We decided to move to Karmiel, a lovely little town about forty kilometers east of Haifa. We would do it on Thursday, 16 December, after Erin had passed her Ulpan final exams and I'd tended to some writing and regained at least a modest ability to walk.

On Friday, 10 December, a *hamsin*, a sand and dust storm with brutally high winds, began to cover the city; it would stay for the better part of three days. It wasn't blinding. But you really couldn't go anywhere, and there was no effective way to keep the dirt out. By Sunday night, 12 December, we were both going stir crazy in an apartment now dusted with grit. Erin finally decided she had to get out for a while.

She came back with a cat. Erin's astonishing with animals, and Be'er-Sheva had no shortage of feral felines to befriend. She'd gotten to know several; indeed, she'd taken up herding cats. But I'd forbidden her to bring any home. There was no way we could keep them and in any event, we were leaving. I looked at her skeptically, then at the head of the shivering feline tucked into her jacket. She explained that this cat had belonged to a former resident of the absorption center, a South African woman who'd abandoned him a few weeks before, when she'd moved. The animal was gentle, apparently had little idea how to survive on his own and was in bad shape from the hamsin. To send him back into the storm would kill him, probably that night. So we took him in, fed him, bathed him, dried him and let him sleep between us. He was a cuddly little thing. We'd taken in feral cats back in Shelton and missed the egocentric affection they bestowed once they were sure they could trust you, i.e., had gotten you properly trained.

The next day, 13 December, we looked for signs of major recovery. There were none. By evening of the next day, Tuesday, he was howling in distress. Again, he slept between us. But it was a restless, painful sleep and by morning he was clearly and desperately ill. Erin took him to a nearby vet to assess his condition and, if necessary, have him euthanized. The vet refused. A nurse hooked the cat up to a subcutaneous rehydration drip, shot him full of antibiotics and gave him some special cat food. "Look," Erin protested, "I just brought the animal here to see what his condition is. He's not my cat."

"It is your destiny to own this cat," said the vet, handing him back and charging only for two cans of food. However, the vet warned, the cat might be suffering from panleukopenia, or feline distemper. If he hadn't been vaccinated, the disease was almost always fatal. Erin was sure he hadn't been vaccinated.

She brought him home. We got on the Net and read up on feline panleukopenia. Within a few hours, the cat was showing all the symptoms. For the next several hours, he grew progressively worse, unable to eat or drink, urinating bright orange, screaming hideously in pain, staggering about. We did what we could to keep him comfortable. We stayed with him, stroking softly and talking. He began slipping in and out of consciousness. I named him Raful, after a tough old Israeli general of the founding generation, and promised him that if he survived we would take him up north. It's better there, I told him.

Come on, Raful. Stay with it, buddy. Get better. You gotta get better. Live, damn you. Live.

At about 2 PM on Wednesday, 15 December, Raful crawled

into a quiet corner of the cool and darkened bathroom that we had converted into a sickroom with a soft bed, food and water for him. An hour or two later, he went into convulsions and died. My hand was upon him, stroking him lightly, as passed from agony to silence. Erin cried. *En passant*, I wondered how soon I might experience the same. I dismissed the thought. We asked ourselves if we'd done the right thing by prolonging his agony, or if dying in a clean, safe place with human warmth might have been worth something. We could not know. We wanted to bury him, just as we'd buried Erin's horse back in America, after Banner had developed severe neurological problems and had to be put down. But it was already dark and we had no shovel, nor really any place to dig a grave. I wrapped the body in a towel that had become his, put him in a cardboard box, sealed it carefully, took it to a dumpster where feline and human scavengers congregated, and commended the time we'd spent together to Soterion. Erin and I left the next morning for Galilee.

They say it's better here.

It is.

Even with the cancer, it is.

We spent a few weeks in the Karmiel absorption center, a place as well-run and livable as the Be'er-Sheva version had been abhorrent. The local bureaucrats and counselors were helpful, considerate and amiable. The local Anglos, a small minority in this heavily Russian city, the same. The local Russians, once you got to know them, the same. We leased a modest apartment. Erin started working part-time. I began looking into the intricacies of starting a business in Israel and maybe finding some at-home work. But I also stayed sick. Finally, I dragged myself to the local clinic and made an appointment with one of their English-speaking physicians. He did what four previous doctors had not: an abdominal exam. He poked, then called in a colleague who also poked. They departed to confer. It didn't take long. Dr. Tal returned to me and said, in essence, "You have a mass. It's huge.

Go to the hospital. Now."

The next four days began on an unstated theme. "Well, Doc, what's my life expectancy?"

"Don't make any plans for the weekend."

Dr. Tal, Israeli-born son of Polish and Hungarian immigrants and a superb family doctor, later told me that he'd suspected advanced pancreatic cancer. The doctors at Carmel Hospital in Haifa settled on an initial diagnosis of acute leukemia. Endless blood and other tests later, including a CT scan, an ultra-sound, a bone marrow biopsy and a subsequent bone marrow aspiration, settled the issue. Non-aggressive lymphoma presenting as leukemia, plus one hell of an enlarged spleen that may have to come out. The lymphoma's not life-threatening. But it's not curable except by a complete bone marrow transplant, not done on people over fifty. Still, it's eminently repressible. So we got busy repressing. They assigned me an oncologist/hematologist, Dr. Mouna, who can only be described as spectacular. We had The Talk. We started chemo.

Time elapsed from emergency-room entry to first treatment and hospital discharge: about ninety-three hours. And never have I been so calm.

The serenity became conscious when I realized that there were two thoughts I hadn't had and would not entertain. The first was, "I'm being punished for non-belief or heresy or apostasy or whatever." I was being attacked by Kreuzias, perhaps. Nothing new there. But punishment implies at least a modicum of legitimacy on the part of the punisher. This I refused to grant. Perhaps others would reach the conclusion that I am being punished, and discern in it both triumphant divine justice and their own gloating vindication. The Godolatrous can be like that. Not my problem. The second thought: I'd not engaged in any of the desperation maneuvers people facing such crises are supposed to undertake. The pleading prayers. The bargaining. The promises. The demands. But there was none of that, just a quiet sense that my deities and I were in this together, that this was something, however it turned out, that we would be doing together. And that my conduct mattered, as something to offer them, as part of the repair of the world, perhaps the repair of the deities of the world.

It was, as the engineers might call it, "proof of concept."

And now that's the working title of the next book. *Soterion: Proof of Concept.* Something longer, more linear and scholarly, perhaps with a bit of personal vocabulary and programmatics. "This is how I did it," offered not as dogma or The One True Way, but as a possible guide to those who might be undertaking their own explorations and creations. This book has been, by design, an exercise in tossing out a lot of stuff rapid-fire, in accordance with that ever-valid principle, "Before you can talk to people, you have to get their attention." If I've gotten anybody's attention, I'd like to offer more. "Come, let us reason together", as a Hebrew prophet once said. He may have been on to something.

Chemo's no fun. But lying still for three or four hours, hooked up to the IV drip, and at home in bed the day after, does offer time for reflection. In my case, it gave me time to conclude the obvious. I'm sixty-two, cancer-stricken, penniless, unemployed, probably unemployable but with no shortage of do-it-yourself opportunities and challenges. I'm alive and happy and blessed. I've learned that it's possible to live and strive to be the kind of human being who can present himself to divinity as someone worthy of consideration and co-operative endeavor. Virtue ethics work. Try it. Perhaps it will meet some needs of your own. But before you try, you might consider judging such changes as you wish to make in yourself according to two criteria. Why *not* start now? And why *not* stop now?

I'm at peace with the fragment of the Jewish deity within me, and with the non-Godolatrous Jewish faith. I have only one question to ask them. "What next?" No, you can't throw anything away. There is no *away*. But human history, including religious history, is very much the story of odd combinations and unlikely recombinances, of things that weren't supposed to come together but did. And do. And may yet again. And may make a difference in the world.

I seek, I find, new personal deities out of the realm of divinity. We ask each other, "What next?" It's an interesting dialogue, simple and clean and worth having. Like all good conversations, it often takes unexpected turns.

I wonder often if indeed it is possible that something like a Soterion sensibility might form among enough of us to craft, not a Messiah, but a common deity to get us through the next few decades. And beyond. The Age now upon us, the Age of the Wars of the Ways, asks, "What does it mean to be human?" and "What does it mean to be more fully human?" Perhaps someday there might be added a third question, "What does it mean to be more than human?" If we can make it that far, perhaps that's what's next.

I also keep up with the news. America, it seems, is tired of America. Tired and angry and confused. Israel, it seems, is tired of Israel. Tired and angry and confused. America and Israel, it seems, are tired of each other. The world, it seems, is tired of both, and also angry and confused. And the planet is weary of us all.

I'm not tired of anything. I'm an American. I'm an Israeli. I'm a Jew. I'm a Soterion Jew. I'm a human being of the age now upon us, with contributions yet to make and, with a little divine co-operation, time left to make them.

Nor am I tired of asking myself, "Is any of this real?" It's a question those of us who take faith, any faith, seriously should never stop asking. In graduate school, I studied the Puritan "morphology of conversion," the process by which those earnest, sturdy people attempted to discern their own predestined eternal fate. The Puritans held that even the most visible of saints must retain some doubt of election, if only as proof of such. If you're absolutely positively sure you're going to Heaven, you're probably not. There's wisdom there.

Others have come up with approaches less honest and less wise. Tertullian: "I believe because it is absurd." No thanks. The world has no further need of absurdity of any kind. Abelard: "I doubt that I may believe." Again, no thanks. Doubt must be more than an intellectual tactic. The old utilitarian/therapeutic, "If it works, it's real." Perhaps. But works at what? Feeling better about yourself should never be a goal in itself. That must be earned. Every day. Earned by effort and demeanor that contributes on earth and may be offered to deity as we come together into whatever combinations we might take. What we do, everything we do, matters. Now, especially. And always, especially.

And on that thought, as the Judeo-Christians might say, "Amen." Or as a Soterion might put it, *Dyat*. The word means, depending upon context, "Amen" or "Listen up, we need to talk" or "Be well." In this context, it means all three, but primarily, "Be well."

Dyat.

ACKNOWLEDGEMENTS

Acknowledgements come in two varieties: personal and intellectual. My greatest debt, both personal and intellectual, is as always to Erin.

Another debt, more recent and ongoing, is to the doctors and staff of the Clalit Clinics in Karmiel and Carmel Hospital in Haifa. You guys are good.

Other personal acknowledgements are not possible here. The reason is that so many of the people who have befriended us or shown us kindness will find much of this book inane, silly, ludicrous, perhaps blasphemous. Their names ought not to be associated with something they would object to so strongly. But thanks to all of you. You know who you are. You two good friends still in Be'er-Sheva, and you the Anglo Grande Dame/Mother Hen of Karmiel, especially.

Intellectually, I should wish to name a few of the writers who have been my guides in various ways. I've only met three of them personally. Jim Stockdale, whom I was honored to get to know. Alvin Kernan, a World War II hero who taught me Shakespeare at Yale and who became my model humanistic professor. And Robert Jay Lifton, whom I interviewed out at Wellfleet long ago, but learned to take seriously only much later. The others include, in no particular order: Jack Miles, Elaine Pagels, Paula Fredricksen, Yehezkel Kaufmann, Amos Oz, Shaye Cohen, William Barclay, Richard Elliott Friedman, Julia Annas, Maxwell Staniforth. Two others who exercised a profound influence, although not the influence they perhaps intended: David Ariel and Elie Wiesel. Others I'm sure I've forgotten. Once again, if I've poached on anyone without proper credit, my apologies. Contact me if you like.

Finally, it should be noted that I have received no financial support of any kind for the direct purpose of writing this book.

But the State of Israel took me and my wife in when the nation of our birth had no further use for us, and for that I am grateful, and will be forever. The policy of the State of Israel is that every citizen and non-citizen resident is medically insured. It is a wise policy. The State of Israel provides an extensive basket of cash and other benefits and services to new immigrants. It guarantees minimum incomes to all citizens after their first year and provides other supports. For these I am also grateful.

Perhaps this book belongs in and to America. But it could only have been written here. And for the time and the freedom to write as I have, I thank the State of Israel, also.

Philip gold
Karmiel, Israel
5 April 2011,
1 Nissan 5771

APPENDIX

I wrote much of this book on a reconditioned PC that my wife picked up in Be'er-Sheva for fifty shekels, about twenty dollars, in a thrift shop. It worked well enough, except that it was programmed for Hebrew and English and couldn't always keep them straight. The drop-downs on my English Word program were in Hebrew and reversed; the machine sometimes compromised on text by running Hebrew script right-to-left but backwards. It also had one of the most creative spell-checkers I've ever encountered. A few examples of "recommended substitutions" of English words for Hebrew transliterations:

Aliyah (Immigration to Israel): Alias.

Emunah (Faith): Eminem.

Halakha (Jewish law): Halvah.

Halakhic (Pertaining to Jewish law): Hitachi.

Haredi (Israeli Ultra-Orthodox): Harried.

Haskala (Jewish Enlightenment): Hackle. Also Haskell, as in Eddie from old TV series "Leave it to Beaver."

HaTikva ("The Hope," Israeli national Anthem): Aptiva.

Ivrit (Hebrew): Irate.

Kelohanu: (Prayer entitled "Eyn Kelohanu, "There is None Like Our God"): Cellophane.

Minyan (Minimum ten adult males for prayer): Minivan, Mishmash.

Parushim (Pharisees, literally, "set apart"): Perish.

Tefillin (Phylacteries worn at prayer): Tail fin; Teflon.

T'shuva (As in, Ba'al T'shuva, one who returns to the faith): Toshiba.

Sinat Hinam (Baseless hatred): Sinat, Sin at; Hinam, Imam.

Yidls (Yiddish term for Jews, not complimentary): Yodels, yells.

And last but certainly not least:
Soterion: Steroid.

ABOUT THE AUTHOR

Philip was raised in Pittsburgh, received his B.A. in History from Yale and his Ph.D. in History from Georgetown University, where he taught for nearly fourteen years. He served eleven years, active and reserve, in the US Marine Corps, retiring (honorary retired reserve, i.e., no pension or benefits) as a major. He has been a fellow of three think tanks; a staff writer for a national news magazine, covering defense and cultural affairs; a syndicated newspaper columnist; and a TV talking head. He does the popular "Progressive FormerCons" blog for the *Seattle Post-Intelligencer*.

Philip is the author of six previous books and over eight hundred articles, columns and reviews. *Yom Kippur Party Goods: Tales of a Soterion Jew* is his seventh. A follow-on volume, *Soterion: Proof of Concept* is planned. It will be more, shall we say, conventionally structured and themed.

Philip currently lives in Karmiel, Israel, with his wife, writer Erin Solaro. His son, Jonathan, is a law student in America.

BOOKS

O is a symbol of the world, of oneness and unity. In different cultures it also means the "eye," symbolizing knowledge and insight. We aim to publish books that are accessible, constructive and that challenge accepted opinion, both that of academia and the "moral majority."

Our books are available in all good English language bookstores worldwide. If you don't see the book on the shelves ask the bookstore to order it for you, quoting the ISBN number and title. Alternatively you can order online (all major online retail sites carry our titles) or contact the distributor in the relevant country, listed on the copyright page.

See our website **www.o-books.net** for a full list of over 500 titles, growing by 100 a year.

And tune in to myspiritradio.com for our book review radio show, hosted by June-Elleni Laine, where you can listen to the authors discussing their books.

mySpiritRadio